HOW TO STUDY

HOW TO STUDY

BY HARRY MADDOX

FAWCETT PREMIER • NEW YORK

CONTENTS

FOREWORD

IN WRITING THIS BOOK I originally intended to cover only those aspects of the psychology of learning which are useful to students. But I found that, although many students know pretty well what they ought to do, they don't do it. So I was led to include chapters on goals and motives, and, also on more general questions of mental and physical health. And I included, for good measure, chapters on writing English and elementary mathematics. This extensive coverage led me outside my own special field of competence. I have therefore submitted various chapters to colleagues who are experts in those fields in which I have no special training or experience. Dr. Ruth Beard read and commented on the chapter on mathematics, and Dr. A. Wilkinson on the chapter on writing English. On the various aspects of physical health I have benefited from many discussions with Dr. J. N. Oliver.* The chapter on group work owes its presence to Professor O. A. Oeser and Dr. S. B. Hammond of Melbourne University, who first demonstrated to me the possibilities of the less didactic methods of education. I am also indebted to Mr. K. J. McAdam, who made detailed and valuable criticisms of parts of the manuscript, and to the publishers for their advice and encouragement when the book was in its early stages. For such defects as remain I am of course solely responsible.

I have benefited from the honest and unvarnished descriptions of their study habits made by my three children, one at the primary, one at the secondary and one at the tertiary stage of education. Discussions with them have, I hope, helped me to avoid some of the academic absurdities which any man who shuts himself up in his study occasionally perpetrates. And I owe most to my wife, for maintaining that domestic order and comfort which facilitate the labors of writing a book.

A number of publishers and authors have kindly given permission for extracts from their works to be included in the book. Specific acknowledgments are made in the text.

* For the chapter on mental health I acknowledge with thanks the kind permission of Professor L. J. Cronbach and his publishers to use an extract from *Educational Psychology*.

HOW TO STUDY

CHAPTER ONE

THE NEED TO LEARN METHODS
OF STUDY

Much are the precious hours of youth misspent
In climbing learning's rugged, steep ascent.

CHURCHILL

YOU may think that study is an individual matter; that methods which suit some individuals will not suit others; and that different methods are appropriate to different subjects. All this is true. Study remains an art. The best methods of learning medieval history will not necessarily be the best methods of learning chemical engineering. But, whatever subject you are studying, there are nevertheless certain general principles which you should know about, and which should enable you to work out your own personal methods and schemes of study more effectively, and with less trial and error.

Success in study depends not only on ability and hard work but also on effective methods of study. Some students can do more work in a given time than others, and do it more easily. This is largely a matter of ability, no doubt, but ability is by no means the only factor. Very roughly the differences between individuals in their capacity for work and study are determined by:

(1) intelligence and special abilities   50–60 per cent
(2) industry, effort and effective study
    methods   30–40 per cent
(3) chance and environmental factors   10–15 per cent

Ability, of course, you must have in order to succeed in higher learning, but ability alone is not enough. Many highly intelligent students fail, particularly in science subjects, because they do insufficient work, or because they have never learned how to study effectively.

Important study skills such as note-taking, reviewing and making plans and schedules have to be learned and practiced, yet very few students get any systematic instruction in these matters. Most have to rely on the study techniques which they learned at school, or to proceed by personal trial and error. Even the most gifted students can seldom discover unaided the most effective ways of studying. Most never improve their methods of work much, either because they fail to realize that it can be done, or because they are not interested in improvement.

Yet a substantial body of knowledge exists on the best ways of studying. This knowledge is derived from a number of sources, among them:

(1) Research investigations which contrast the study habits of good and poor students.
(2) The experimental psychology of learning.
(3) Actual empirical studies of the relative effectiveness of different methods of study.
(4) Industrial studies of the conditions of work efficiency.
(5) Common sense and logic, and a certain consensus among students of the learning process that some methods are more effective than others.

Applying Research Findings to Your Own Study Methods

Take a question which must concern all students: What is the most effective method of learning from textbooks? Several methods are possible, e.g.:

(1) simple reading and rereading.
(2) underlining the main points and important details in the text.
(3) reading and then making brief outline notes.

Actual research studies of the effectiveness of these methods, as judged by examination success, have in fact been done on quite a large scale. Method (3) turned out to be best, but only if the text was read over first in order to get the general sense, and if the notes were made in the student's own words. Without some practice and training in note-taking, method (3) was actually inferior to method (1).

Now it is true that this research was done on high school students, the subject being history. You may wonder, and with some reason, whether these findings can be applied to more advanced students and to subjects other than history. But at least, if you are concerned with this question, you should know of this research. For it does suggest that, in the absence of contrary evidence, method (3) is likely to be the most promising one for you to try out. In other words, although no one can tell you exactly how you should study your particular subjects, you should be able to work out your own methods more intelligently if you know something of the relevant research findings. Even good students do not usually know enough about study methods, and could improve their performance by thinking about, and applying to their own work, the research findings which are set out in this book.

Regular Class Attendance

There have been a number of investigations of the differences in study habits which distinguish good students from poor students. One careful study did find the following differences between successful and failing students:

	Successful Students	Failing Students
Average classroom hours per week	27	18
Percentage of total work time devoted to a regular program	57	49
Fullness of lecture notes (100 = notes written out in full)	64	47
Percentage reviewing notes the same day	21	8

Fig. 1. Differences in the study habits of successful and failing students

The better students put in more classroom hours, and worked to a more regular program. They took fuller lecture notes, and were more likely to review their notes the same day.

It is clear that the failing students must have cut some of

their classes. Failure to attend classes is one obvious cause of poor performance. In another investigation, carried out in a college, the number of times each student had been absent from class was plotted against his subsequent marks. There was a definite relationship between class attendance and marks obtained.

Those who frequently cut classes were less likely to get high marks than those who were regular in their attendance. Attendance requirements differ a great deal from one institution to another. But most institutions place emphasis on training, and usually insist on class attendance. In general, requirements in science departments are more rigid than in arts.

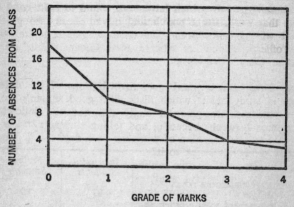

Fig. 2. The influence of class absences on marks obtained

Many college teachers do not call a roll or enforce attendance at their lectures, but you would be unwise to conclude from this that you need not go to them, and even more unwise to conclude that you can stay away from practical classes or tutorials. Although reading a textbook may sometimes be an adequate substitute for attending a lecture, there is no substitute for practical work or tutorials. Moreover, there are many subjects in which continuity of treatment is essential. In order to progress, the professor assumes that you have mastered the material and methods which he dealt with the previous week. It is annoying for him to have to retrace his steps and repeat explanations for the benefit of those who have been absent without good cause. If this happens often he will be only human if he takes a dislike to the truants, and marks them down in examinations. Some teachers even regard repeated absence from their classes as a personal slight. In any case, you should find out what the local customs are. In most places you will find that it is politic to apologize to your teachers for any unavoidable absences.

Not all the research evidence is equally valuable, it has to be confessed. The attempt to locate the study habits which differentiate between good and poor students has not been very successful, because the results which hold good for one college or university seldom seem to apply outside that particular college or university. However, here are some questionnaire items which have been found to hold good on more than one student population. If you check through the list it will give you some idea of how you compare with the "official version" of what a good student should do.

QUESTIONNAIRE
HOW GOOD A STUDENT ARE YOU?

	Preferred Answer
1. Do you have a plan of work for each day?	Yes
2. If so, do you stick to it?	Yes
3. Do you have trouble settling down to work at the beginning of a study period?	No
4. Do you get your work in on time?	Yes
5. Do you find your work interesting?	Yes
6. Do you participate in class discussions?	Yes
7. Do you try to sit towards the back of the classroom?	No
8. When you have trouble with your work do you talk over the matter with your teacher?	Yes
9. Do you make a preliminary survey before reading a chapter in detail?	Yes
10. Do you skip tables and graphs in your reading?	No
11. Do you keep your notes for one subject all together?	Yes
12. Do you usually take your lecture notes in outline form?	Yes
13. Do you make simple charts, diagrams or tables of your own to summarize material in your reading?	Yes

14. Do you have difficulty in expressing yourself in
    writing?   No
15. If an examination is given unexpectedly do you
    fail or get a low mark?   No
16. Do you sit up late preparing for an examination?   No
17. Do you do most of your reviewing for a course
    the night before the examination?   No
18. Do you get enough sleep?   Yes
19. Do you have certain hours that you regularly
    spend in recreation?   Yes
20. On your study desk is there a clear unlittered
    space about 2 feet by 4 feet?   Yes

How to Improve

To be an efficient student you must also be an efficient person, and manage other aspects of your life in a sensible fashion. This means planning your finances, living arrangements, diet, dress and exercise, and all the other details of your personal life, as well as attending your classes regularly, being punctual and getting your work done at the right time.

To improve your general efficiency you can:

(1) increase your mental vigor, by improving your general health.
(2) improve the direction and method of work by planning and distributing your study in an efficient manner.
(3) decrease the forces which inhibit work by developing interest and motivation.
(4) relieve worry and excitement by resolving personal conflicts.

Factual advice is much easier to give on the first two lines of attack than on the third and fourth. You can readily learn the technique of effective study. It is much harder to work up interest in a subject which you find uninteresting, although, even here, some practical advice can be given.

If you are to work effectively on your own you must have a sustained interest in your work, and learn to use your time wisely. The main difference between studying at school and studying after you leave school lies in the closeness of supervision. At school for every two hours of work in the classroom there will be about an hour of homework or private study; in college, for every hour of work in the classroom, one or two hours of private study. In college there are no set hours for private study, and you can do as you please in the free hours between classes, or even stay away from your lectures and classes altogether. You will seldom be set work which you have to prepare for the next meeting of the class, but instead will be given a few larger assignments to be done in the course of the term. There will very seldom be any class time set aside for reviewing, the assumption being that you can look after this yourself. In general, it is left to you to decide how much work you do and when you do it, and the day of reckoning, in the shape of an examination, may not come until the end of the academic year. You must therefore work steadily towards rather distant goals. To do this you must be interested in what you are doing, and be able to arrange for yourself many aspects of your work which you may previously have taken for granted, and not thought about very much. Research, in fact, shows that the main difficulties in beginning a course of higher studies are:

(1) In budgeting time, and
(2) In coping with unfamiliar methods of work.

You should, therefore, see the need for learning all you can about the skills and techniques which make for efficient study. If you can work out for yourself an efficient system of study you will be able to do your work better with less effort, and in less time.

Efficient methods of study are worth learning not only for your immediate purposes of study, but because your habits of work will stay with you all your life. Those who do well in academic work usually do equally well afterwards in business or in the professions. No doubt the same abilities and personality characteristics underlie both study and later work, but efficient methods of work also contribute to success in both fields.

Is Advice on How to Study Effective?

Many colleges run courses on how to study. Most of the investigations of the effectiveness of such courses have shown that they do produce positive results. At first these courses were given only to students who were in difficulty, but it subsequently appeared that all students benefited from them —in fact the better students improved more than the poor students.

These courses usually involve lectures, discussions and individual tuition. Lectures on how to study generally turn out to be rather ineffective. They are ineffective because the advice given may not be accepted, or because the student cannot see how to apply the information to his own particular case. A book on how to study has some advantages over a lecture. A book is always available for reference. It is, moreover, often easier to accept advice from an impersonal source.

No one has ever proved experimentally that reading a book on how to study leads to improvement, but those students who have read such books usually say that they found them helpful. The crucial question is whether you put into practice the advice given. There is a big difference between knowing what you should do and actually doing it. Many students know that they should work regularly, review their notes, etc., but they don't do these things. For this reason this book starts out with chapters on how to plan your time and how to acquire habits of work.

Motives for Study

It is much easier to work in a sustained and systematic fashion if you have a definite vocational goal or a strong interest in your subject. In an investigation at one university, mental tests were given to students on entry, and their test scores compared with subsequent examination marks. By this means it was possible to identify a group of over-achievers (who did well although their test scores were below average) and a group of under-achievers (who failed although their test scores were above average). Nearly half the under-achievers were found to have weak or unsatisfactory motives, whereas most of the over-achievers had a definite vocational goal or strong intellectual interest in their course:

	Definite vocational goal or intellectual interest per cent	Weak or unsatisfactory motives per cent
Over-achievers	88	12
Under-achievers	57	43

Fig. 3. The motives of over-achievers and under-achievers

Thus lack of adequate motivation is an important cause of academic failure.

In the same investigation it was found that about a quarter of the under-achievers, but very few of the over-achievers, had job aspirations which were incompatible with their present courses. It is better to make a positive choice of a course of study, than to take it up because it seems the only course open or because all alternative courses are disliked.

Vocational Choice

Many older people look back on their lives, and regret that they did not obtain some good vocational guidance when they were about 16 years of age. Is there any way of deciding whether you have chosen a suitable course of study? There is no simple answer to this question. But if you enjoy your work, are interested in it, and are not strongly attracted by other professions and courses of training, you have probably chosen reasonably well. It is, of course, very common to have doubts, and to consider alternative courses, in the early years of higher study. In some colleges as many as 40 per cent of students change their vocational choice in the course of their studies. In a sample of eminent men, it was found that only one-third had chosen their profession on leaving school.

Probably it should be made easier than it is at present to transfer from one course of study to another. The hard fact is, however, that this nearly always means at least an extra year of study. Radical changes are therefore not to be lightly undertaken. Remember that "the grass is always greener on the other side of the fence"—until you get there.

The difficulty confronting most young people of good general ability is that they would probably be equally successful in a wide range of professions. Just as it is a romantic fallacy to suppose that there is a single "right" person for everyone to marry, so it is a fallacy to suppose that there is a single right job for every person. Aptitudes, which are largely the product of training anyway, are not specific to particular occupations, and are therefore an inadequate basis for vocational choice.

Rational choice of occupation is extremely difficult because choice often has to be made around the age of 14 years, in the schoolroom, remote from the world of work. At this age choice tends to be made on the basis of the parents' ideas, and on the basis of supposed aptitude for school subjects. Apparent aptitude and interest at this age are very insecure bases of choice. The relation between school marks in any subject and subsequent performance in that subject is not very high. Often the supposed aptitude is as much a matter of accident or teaching method as of any permanent ability, and interests in adolescence are notoriously unstable.

Choosing higher courses of study solely on the basis of school subject performance has two consequences:

(1) Higher courses in "school" subjects such as English, French, geography, physics and chemistry tend to be overcrowded, while the applied and social sciences find it hard to recruit enough students of quality.
(2) Many students take courses of higher study without adequately considering whether they will lead to congenial work.

The "reality" factors concerning occupations which tend to be overlooked at the age at which choice is made are:

The nature of the duties involved
Earnings
Hours and regularity of employment
Typical places of employment
The probable need for workers in the occupation

The Meaning of Efficiency

This book contains a great deal of advice. Some of it you will, I hope, accept. Some of it you will regard as good practice, but impracticable in your own case. Some of it you will disagree with and reject. But at least you should be led to think about your own methods of study, and to attempt to improve them. If the advice given seems occasionally earnest and moralistic, I can only say that it is very hard to avoid a high moral tone in a book of this sort.

The key word throughout the book is efficiency, a word which is often suspect because it suggests time and motion study, the rationalization of work procedure, and the rather dreary fractionization of tasks into simple repetitive sequences, which characterizes much of modern industrial work. As all forms of higher learning depend on self-education and on self-sustained effort, study procedures cannot and should not be reduced to an excessively mechanical routine.

By efficiency I shall mean getting the maximum learning and retention for the least expenditure of energy and effort. Human efficiency is, of course, an extremely complex problem. It is impossible to treat the human individual in the same way that an engineer treats an engine, in terms of the amount of work done in relation to the energy consumed. As the human individual works he expends energy and effort, but he may also become fatigued or bored with his task. He may wish he was doing something else and feel irritated and frustrated. On the positive side he may enjoy his work and obtain satisfaction when a task has been well done. Many factors have to be considered in assessing the "cost" of work to the individual.

In spite of the complexity of the matter, however, you should benefit from stepping back and taking a detached view of yourself and your efforts. Each person doubtless is unique, but there are also great similarities between persons, particularly between those who have been molded by the same kind of social training and education. The same general laws of learning and remembering apply to all human organisms. Therefore you should be able to apply some of them to your own case.

This book starts with some advice on how to make plans and schedules. Many students have difficulty in allocating their time sensibly among the many activities which make some call on them. Some students say they are happier when they feel free to work as the mood takes them. They would probably be happier still doing no work at all. The fact is that a certain self-discipline and regularity are demanded by any extended course of study.

Effort can only be sustained over a period of some years by developing regular habits, and by having goals and motives appropriate to the task. The next chapter should give you some understanding of how habits are set up, and what you can do to develop motives.

The following chapters deal with a series of study skills. A well known "system" of study is explained, and chapters follow on reading, note-taking, and taking examinations, on thinking and group work. Basic skills in English and mathematics are presented so that you may brush up your knowledge of these subjects if you feel the need. Finally there are three chapters on the general conditions governing health, both physical and mental. Each chapter can be read separately, as you feel the need to learn more about each topic. But you are advised to read through the whole book quickly at first, and to mark those portions that you need to return to, and to study more thoroughly.

OTHER BOOKS ON STUDY

These include:

Bennett, M.E.	*College and Life.*	McGraw-Hill, New York, 1952.
Bird, C. and Bird, D.M.	*Learning More by Effective Study.*	Appleton-Century-Crofts, New York, 1945.
Morgan, C.T. and Deese, J.	*How to Study.*	McGraw-Hill, New York, 1957.
Robinson, F.P.	*Effective Study.*	Harper and Row, New York, 1961.

CHAPTER TWO

PLANS AND SCHEDULES

In studies, whatsoever a man commandeth upon
himself, let him set hours for it.

BACON

BY far the most common difficulty in study is simple
failure to get down to regular concentrated work. This difficulty is much greater for those who do not work with a
plan and have no regular routine of study. Many students muddle along, doing a bit of this subject or that, as
the mood takes them, or letting their set work pile up until
the last possible moment.

Few students work to a set schedule. They say that if
they did construct a schedule for themselves they would not
keep to it, or would have to alter it constantly, since they
can never predict from one day to the next what their
activities will be.

No doubt some temperaments take much more kindly to
a regular routine than others. There are many who shy
away from the self-regimentation of a weekly schedule, and
dislike being tied down to a definite program of work. Many
able students claim that they work in cycles. When they become interested in a topic they work on it intensively for
three or four days at a time. On other days they avoid work
completely. It has to be confessed that we do not fully understand the complexities of the motivation to work. Most
people over about 25 years of age have become conditioned
to a work routine, and the majority of really productive
workers set aside regular hours for the more important aspects of their work. The "tough-minded" school of workers
is usually very contemptuous of the idea that good work can
only be done spontaneously, under the influence of inspiration. That most energetic of authors, Anthony Trollope,
wrote: "There are those . . . who think that the man who

works with his imagination should allow himself to wait till inspiration moves him. When I have heard such doctrine preached, I have hardly been able to repress my scorn."

Not many people are gifted with Trollope's great energy and physical strength, but he was undoubtedly right in declaring that a person can always do the work for which he is fitted if he will give himself the habit of regarding regular daily work as a normal condition of his life. Many creative writers have in fact disciplined themselves to perform a daily stint. The great Italian dramatist, Alfieri, even made his servant tie him to his study table.

Those who believe that they need only work and study as the fit takes them have a mistaken belief either in their own talent or in the value of "freedom". Freedom from restraint and discipline leads to unhappiness rather than to "self-expression" or "personality development". Our society insists on regular habits, time-keeping and punctuality, and whether we like it or not, if we mean to make our way in society we have to comply with its demands. We need not stick too rigidly to plans and schedules, but plans there must be. Otherwise effort is wasted and time is dribbled away to no purpose. A sensible routine of work, so far from destroying spontaneity or creativity, should in fact, by reducing to a minimum the effort of coping with the humdrum activities of life, actually foster the best conditions for creative work.

The other obstacles to the regular planning of study are the many distractions of student life: new sports and activities, novel surroundings, friendships and love affairs, organizations, clubs, societies and sometimes excesses of conviviality. You need to find a sensible balance between all these competing demands on your time. To do this you need to be quite clear about your goal. The primary goal of any sort of higher study must be scholarship and professional qualification. The other things, friendship, sports, societies, discussions on the nature of the universe, and having a good time, are no doubt important and traditional parts of student life; but they are secondary to your primary goal of study.

The Advantages of a Schedule

Plans and schedules are even more necessary to the student than to others because, outside the classroom, he is free, within limits, to do what he will. Farmers, businessmen, lawyers, doctors and professional men of all kinds must work to a schedule and plan the best use of their time, but their times are largely decided by factors over which they have no control. A student's work is not so closely controlled by external circumstances, and for that very reason, set hours of work should be arranged so that study does not become spasmodic.

The advantages of a schedule are the savings in time and effort, and the efficiency which results from taking an overall view of your total work load. Without a schedule you are likely to spend much time in indecision—in making up your mind when and what to study, in getting together the necessary books and materials and in getting into the appropriate frame of mind for productive work. Much mental energy is needlessly consumed in trying to choose between alternatives and in screwing up your resolution to work. According to William James: "There is no more miserable human being than one in whom nothing is habitual but indecision, and for whom the lighting of every cigar, the drinking of every cup, the times of rising and going to bed every day, and the beginning of every bit of work, are subjects of express volitional deliberation." To avoid this unhappy state we should make automatic and habitual as many useful actions as we can. Handing over the details of our daily life to habit frees the higher powers of mind for their proper work.

The second advantage is in the proper use of time. It is fatally easy to dribble time away. If you do not impose set hours on yourself you are more than likely to spend the time when you should be studying in watching T.V., reading a magazine, conversing idly over the tea- and coffee-cups, or in doing any of those hundred and one things which weak students are ready to do rather than get down to work. If you have a schedule and mean to stick to it, it has all the force of a law which must not be disobeyed, and in time adherence to it becomes effortless, and you begin to regard it as a natural part of your life.

But perhaps the biggest saving comes from intelligently dovetailing your various activities; in making sure that you do each piece of work at the best possible time; and, eventually, in the confidence and sense of competence which comes from regular daily work. As Trollope said, "A small daily task, if it be really daily, will beat the labors of a spasmodic Heracles."

Regularity, then, is the ideal that you should aim at. Even if you decide not to work to a detailed schedule, you should at least set aside certain hours for study and plan to do a certain quantity of work each week.

Examination of your Present Routine

Before you begin to plan out your work, however, you need to know in detail exactly how you do spend your time. For this purpose you should keep a minute account of your waking activities for one or two working days or, better still, for a week. Do not regard this as trivial or as a waste of time. Nothing is unimportant if you are compelled to attend to it every day of your life, such as dressing, washing, eating breakfast and getting to your place of work. It is highly unlikely that you know with any exactitude just how you do spend your time in a typical day. Therefore keep a careful record, such as this example:

MONDAY

Action	Until	Duration
Sleep	7:00	8 hrs.
Lie in bed	7:30	30 mins.
Shave	7:40	10
Read newspaper	8:00	20
Dress	8:15	15
Breakfast	8:30	15
Read newspaper	8:40	10
Toilet	8:50	10
Search for notebook	9:00	10
Walk to bus	9:05	5
Wait for bus	9:15	10
Travel to work	9:45	30
Talk to friends	10:00	15
Attend lecture	11:00	60 etc.

(This sample record, by no means unusual, shows a rather poor organization of time. The person is awake at 7 a.m., but three hours elapse before he does any work.)

When you have kept the record for some days you may like to try and classify your waking activities and to add up the time spent under each heading.

Action	Mon.	Tues.	Wed.	Thurs.	Fri.	Total
Sleep						
Meals						
Classes						
Study						
Clubs and societies						
Social activities						
Sports						
Travel						
Other necessary actions						
Time wasted						

From the totals you can then calculate the percentage of your time spent under each heading. The questions you will naturally ask yourself are:

(1) Does the overall distribution of time correspond to my needs and purposes?
(2) Is enough time spent on study?
(3) Is any particular action taking up too much time?
(4) Do I waste too much time, and when and how does this occur?

Long-Term Plans and Weekly Schedules

In tackling any course of study you should make for yourself (1) a long-term plan embracing the year's work, planning even further ahead when necessary and (2) a weekly schedule, constructed afresh each week.

For the long-term plan you must find out all about the various syllabuses you will have to cover, the textbooks which you must read and learn, the practical work and other requirements which you have to fulfill. Set yourself "deadlines" for completing important pieces of work, such as essays, practical notebooks or investigations. Always plan ahead as far as you possibly can—lengthen your time perspective and don't live from hand to mouth. Of course these long-term plans may have to be revised from time to time, but you should have a broad general picture of your year's work. You may not be able to elaborate these long-term plans until you have had some weeks' experience of your courses, but do not neglect them. More than any other factor they distinguish the good student from the bad. All good teachers provide their students with outlines of their courses

at the outset, so that they "know where they are going". If
any of your teachers fail to do this, you should tactfully
ask them to do so.

A detailed schedule needs to be made out at the beginning
of each week, in keeping with the changing requirements of
your courses, and in the light of your experience. The weekly
schedule allows flexibility but at the same time ensures that
you will be prepared to do each piece of work at the best
possible time. Many students intend to study on set evenings,
but are only too ready to cancel or postpone their work on
a small pretext. If you have a definite schedule you will be
less likely to procrastinate.

To make a realistic and effective schedule needs a certain
amount of self-knowledge. It is no use making grandiose
plans of work that you are never likely to be able to put into
effect. Usually you need only schedule your set classes and
private study time. Your other activities can be left to themselves, provided that you leave a reasonable amount of time
for exercise, sports and social and cultural activities. To try
and plan every hour of your life would be pedantic and un-
workable.

The Amount of Study Needed

As regards the total amount of study time, it is useful to
know roughly how much work most students actually do.
The average study time is about 40 hours a week. Arts students generally have about 15 classroom hours a week, and
spend about 25 in private study—reading, writing essays,
etc. Science students spend up to 30 hours a week in the
classroom and laboratories, but usually do not do more than
15 hours of private study. These are only average figures of
course. Within the general framework each person has to
determine for himself how much time to spend in private
study, but almost certainly your total hours should lie within
the 30–50 hour range. Clever students work faster than
those of less ability, but two equally clever students may
spend very different amounts of time in study. One, satisfied
with just getting by, may average only a few hours a week;
the other, driven by intellectual curiosity or a desire to excel,
may read widely and do far more than the minimum requirements.

It should be said that most students overrate their speed
of work and the amount that they can accomplish in a set

time. Hence it is good practice to allow a few extra hours as a "safety factor". At the same time your hours of work should not be excessive. Industrial studies show that if excessively long hours are worked over a long period, output actually declines and becomes less than the output that could be achieved in shorter hours. Your total working hours will have to exceed about 70 a week, however, before you need start worrying about this!

The Common Pattern of Working Hours

If you are a full-time student, the pattern of set classes into which you must fit your private study periods is usually something like this: from Monday to Friday you will have set classes for most of the morning hours, with occasional free periods between the lectures and classes. The afternoons will be taken up with practical or laboratory periods in science, and left rather more free in arts. There is a period each day from about 4–7 p.m. when not a great deal of work is done—this is the usual time for social gatherings, clubs and societies. If you usually start going to bed around 11 p.m. this means that the greater part of your private study will have to be done in the weekday evenings between about 7 and 11 p.m. Saturday mornings are worked by many science but by few arts departments. Saturday afternoons are, by custom, set aside for sports and entertainment; Sundays for thought, relaxation, outings or for religious observance.

It follows that the most natural arrangement for arts students is to plan their 25 hours of study time to fall in the afternoons (4x2 hours) and evenings (4x3 hours) on Mondays, Tuesdays, Thursdays and Fridays, finding the odd five hours in free morning periods or on weekends. Science students will plan their 15 hours of study (assuming they are fully occupied with practical work in the afternoons) to fall in the evenings (4x3 hours) on Mondays, Tuesdays, Thursdays and Fridays, making up the rest at odd morning hours or on the weekend.

Unless you are an exceptional individual, you will be wise not to depart too far from this general pattern of hours. It is usually a mistake to set yourself a strenuous program of work on Saturday evenings, for example, when the rest of the world is out for enjoyment. The pull of counter-attractions will be greater and more energy will be consumed in concentrating on your task. Conversely, if you keep to the common pattern of work, the sight of others studying or the mere knowledge that they are doing so, facilitates your own task.

Avoid Late Hours

A common departure from this sensible arrangement is to start work late, possibly after a round of social activities, and to work through until the early hours of the morning. Some students claim that they can do their best work late at night, undistracted, while others sleep. If these late hours become habitual, however, it is clearly not very easy to get up and be alert and attentive at a lecture next morning, unless indeed you also take a siesta each afternoon. Often a false glamour attaches to this working into the night and performing a prodigious amount of labor. Work done under the midnight oil often fails to stand up to the cold light of day. As an occasional technique for completing some big task, working into the night may be all very well, but most regular classes, where much of the important instruction is given, take place in the mornings; and to be fresh and alert in the mornings you must have had a good night's sleep.

Diurnal Variations in Efficiency

Most people believe that they work best at certain hours of the day. There is some truth in this, but it is still possible to work effectively at any hour. Studies of industrial output show that, where an eight-hour day is worked, production rises to a maximum during both morning and afternoon, tailing off slightly in the morning and more markedly in the late afternoon.

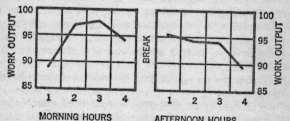

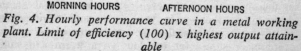

Fig. 4. *Hourly performance curve in a metal working plant. Limit of efficiency (100) x highest output attainable*

In the early morning there is a "warming up period" before full output is attained. The diurnal variation in output is, however, quite small. Factory work is different from study, of course, and you should not think that there is a "typical" curve of daily work which will resemble exactly the course of your own daily working efficiency.

The decline in mental work towards the end of the day is certainly less than the decline in manual work. In one well-known experiment a student worked continuously for twelve hours a day doing mental multiplication of four-figure numbers by four-figure numbers, such as 7,241x2,818. The experiment continued for four days. The rate of work did become slower towards the end of the twelve-hour day, but the work was continued uninterrupted for twelve hours each day, the work on the fourth day being better than the work on the first day.

Work curves do suggest, however, that morning output is higher than afternoon, and certainly schools, colleges and universities all put their most strenuous and demanding work into the mornings. Hence it is only sensible to ensure that you are fit and alert for morning work. If you are not, examine your habits of sleep, diet and exercise, to see if you cannot become an early riser. In other words, if you are sluggish in the mornings, don't regard this as the result of some inherent defect in your physiology, but look for the causes and try and alter them. In my view the morning hours are easily the most valuable, and, for most people, the best time for serious work. Therefore it is worth making every effort to see that your morning hours are not frittered away. Don't do minor chores in the mornings that can just as easily be done later in the day. If necessary, organize yourself so as to make an early start as easy as possible. Small things like laying out your clothes in readiness for the next day, preparing the breakfast table the night before, etc., not only save time in the early morning, but enable you to get through the necessary preliminaries to the working day with less effort and hurry. A little forethought before you retire to bed often enables you to make a flying start the next day.

Similarly if you find that you become tired and sleepy in either the afternoons or the evenings, try and find the cause —which must be either in you or in your environment. Often it is too heavy a meal at the wrong time of day or lack of exercise, or sitting for too long in a warm and stuffy room. Remember, too, that alcohol depresses brain action If you are unwise enough to take alcohol on your study nights, your condition is bound to be unfavorable for work.*

Your aim should be, then, never to be the slave of the slight diurnal variations in efficiency to which we are all subject. By all means do as much important work as you can in the mornings, but take practical steps to overcome the conditions which promote fatigue (which is largely subjective) at other times of the day.

Filling in the Schedule

The next questions which arise concern how best to apportion your various tasks within the periods of time which you have set aside for study, to decide on the best length for individual "units" of study, on rest intervals, and on the amount of time to allocate to each subject.

Since you cannot at first be quite sure how much time to allocate to the various subjects of your course, you must make the best guesses you can. If you find some particular subject difficult, allot more time to it than the others. Do not neglect it in favor of another subject which you find easier or more interesting. Make a fresh schedule at the beginning of each week.

The best time to write up your lectures or experiments is as soon as possible after the event. If you have to keep a practical notebook, for example, it is a good rule to write it up *the same day,* when the material is fresh in your mind. If you set it aside it will only take you longer to do in the end. Likewise the best time for the first review of your lecture notes is immediately after the lecture, or at least on the same day.

The Length of Individual Study "Units"

The length of your individual study "units" deserves serious thought. The most efficient arrangement depends on:

(1) the complexity and size of the task.
(2) the characteristics of the individual learner.

* The effect of the diet and exercise is dealt with more fully in Chapter 13.

If you have a large task such as writing a long essay, it may be uneconomic to work on it for half an hour or even for an hour at a time. Time is needed for you to assemble your materials and your thoughts, and to "warm up" to the task. By the time you have got your ideas straight it may be time to stop—before you have made any tangible progress.

Usually, therefore, if you have an experiment to report or an essay to write, it is best to complete it at a single sitting, once you have assembled all the necessary materials, provided that it can be done in a total of 2 or 3 hours.

Individuals differ in the ease to which they can take up a fresh task, work on it, and then turn to something else. If you find it easy to switch from one subject to another, you will be able to work efficiently in smaller "units" than those who not only take a long time to get started on a task, but also find it hard to stop thinking about it afterwards.

A very common difficulty, not only for such "perseverators", but for everyone, is to find enough long uninterrupted periods in which to perform those tasks which cannot be completed in a single hour.

The single hour is the common unit of instruction for lectures, and may well be as long as most people care to work on a single subject, without an intervening rest period. For practical work, on the other hand, 2- or 3-hour sessions are usual. Probably for many tasks and for most people, a working period of about an hour, followed by a few minutes' rest or relaxation is quite effective. Some individuals much prefer to switch to a different task after about an hour. As a general rule, for reading, note-taking and learning from books, an hour is a suitable work unit; but, particularly as you advance to the more complex and difficult aspects of a subject, larger work units may be more effective. Most university students prefer work periods of 2–3 hours for many forms of private study.

Value of Rest Periods

There are optimum periods of work and rest for every task and for every individual. In the course of study, rest periods are invaluable. Although the speed and accuracy of mental work actually declines very little, boredom, distractability and dissatisfaction with the task tend to set in after about two hours, if there is no break. During a session of continuous work on the same task, rest periods should be short in relation to the work period—of the order of 5 minutes or so. If longer rests are taken momentum will be lost and possibly considerable effort may be required before you become warmed up to the task again. A rest should be taken whenever you feel that you are slowing down and making errors. After working on a task for some time, a growing distaste for it occurs, together with an increasing desire to stop work altogether. But if you resolve, instead of doing this, to rest and relax for 10 minutes and then to get back to work, the desire to get down to the task again often returns and you get your "second wind".

A change in activity or posture during the rest are desirable, such as walking around the room, stretching your arms, etc. Rest intervals between different tasks may well be longer —about 10 or 15 minutes. Then a short, brisk walk outside, or some light refreshment, often serve to restore your energies to their former level. In manual work 5 or 10 minutes' rest each hour is beneficial, and you should not need to break off much more frequently than this. Remember that much of mental fatigue springs from boredom of lack of interest rather than any real inability to continue with the task.

In general, then, it is sensible to take 15-minute breaks at convenient times between tasks, and smaller breaks of a few minutes in the course of a task. It is much better to take a definite rest interval and then get back to hard work, than to work half-heartedly for too long.

Vacations

In most colleges and institutions of higher education the session extends for only part of the year. What is the best way of using the vacations?

In the past students were supposed to supplement their studies by wide and extensive reading in the vacations. Nowadays many students find it necessary to work in order to make enough money to live on. The first question that arises, then, is should you take paid work in the vacations?

Although some authorities think that students should study in the vacation, and not take on paid outside employment, particularly manual labor, surveys show that neither those students who take employment, nor those who do not, study very much in the vacations. In my view there is everything to be said for working in the vacations, particularly if the work bears some relation to study: engineers and chemists should work in industry, technicians on farms, social workers as nurses, language students abroad, etc. Academic learning is only one sort of learning: students and their teachers are always in danger of getting out of touch with the larger world of industry, trade and agriculture. Everyone should explore the society in which he lives, and get firsthand knowledge of how people live in social classes other than his own. There is no evidence to show that those who take paid employment in the vacations do any worse at their studies than those who do not. On the contrary, research shows that students who take part-time employment are more earnest and more purposeful, and better students than those who do not.

There is substantial agreement that people who take longish vacations away from their work are more productive workers than those who do not. Certainly many businessmen claim that they can do twelve months' work in nine months, but not in twelve months. Work should not become an obsession. At the same time my view is that the sort of idle seaside vacation which may suit a tired factory worker is not the best sort of vacation for a student. Something more active and purposeful is required, such as walking, mountaineering, work-camps, expeditions and field studies.

In general, the common advice to "get away from it all" and make a complete break from your work seems to be good advice. You should, however, set aside a part of the vacation for reviewing and for going over parts of your work that you may have fallen behind with.

The Distribution of Practice

Taking a long view, and considering the course of learning over a period of weeks or months, spaced (or "distributed") learning sessions are more effective than "massed" practice. Both long-term retention and understanding will be better if you spread out your learning, rather than try and cram it into a single session. For instance, if you have a total of three hours in which to learn about a topic, it will usually be better to study it, say, for an hour on one evening, for a further hour a few days later, and for a third time a week or ten days later, than to work on it for three hours in one evening and then do no further work on it. In distributed learning each learning session serves to reinforce your knowledge, and you have more time to think about it and organize it. There is a limit to the amount of information that can be properly assimilated at any one time: time is needed for thinking and for consolidating your knowledge. <u>The worst form of learning, both from the point of view of understanding and of long-term retention, is</u> cramming before examinations: you merely fill your head with a mass of ill-digested facts which are very soon forgotten. The evils of cramming are dealt with at greater length in the chapter on preparing for examination.

Summary

By now it should be clear that you can construct a flexible schedule which will not tie you to a rigid routine, will save you time and effort, and enable you to keep pace with the requirements of your study. The thought and planning involved in constructing a good workable schedule are repaid many times over. Here are the main steps again:

(1) Detailed examination of all your waking activities. Analysis of your daily routine, to ensure that the necessary "maintenance" activities such as meals, travel, shopping, etc., do not take up too much of your time.

(2) Planning as far ahead as possible, so that you have a general picture of what lies before you.

(3) Decision on the total amount of weekly study time you need to perform. Your total hours of work, including classes, should be around 40, and should almost certainly not lie outside the range of 30–50 hours.

(4) Decision on when to carry out your private study. Conform if you can to the common pattern of working hours: do your important work in the mornings, study for four evenings each week and leave the weekends relatively free. But don't think that there are certain hours of the day when you can't work. Fatigue is mostly subjective and diurnal variations in efficiency are small.

(5) At the beginning of each week, plan your study times for the whole week. Flexibility enters here. Observe these principles:

(a) Do each piece of work at the best time. Go over your lecture notes the same day. Write up experiments when they are still fresh in your mind.

(b) Try and discover the best length of study period for your various tasks. A sizeable task is often best tackled in a single 2- or 3-hour session.

(c) Plan for rest periods between tasks, and shorter rest intervals in the course of a task.

Keep a Diary or Journal

It is useful practice to keep a diary or journal. This is best done in a large exercise book—pocket diaries are useless for this purpose. Keeping a daily record will only take five or ten minutes a day; and in summing up each day's activities, you have a permanent record of your plans in action. You will find that you have good days and bad days, victories and failures. On one day you may be buoyed up with hopes on the very same grounds that give you cause for anxiety on the next. We are all subject to these ebbs and flows of feeling, so it is as well to recognize it, and to determine to stick doggedly to our self-appointed tasks, even when we appear to be making little progress.

CHAPTER THREE

MOTIVES AND HABITS

Continuity of thought upon one single thing, and the suppression of every source of distraction, multiply in an extraordinary way the value of time.

ALFIERI

THE quality of your work counts just as much as the quantity —in fact it is pointless to put in hours of study if they are not effective. We all know we can accomplish more in an hour of concentrated work than in a whole evening spent dawdling over a textbook, without any real effort and intention to learn. How can your concentration be improved? Basically you must be interested in the course you are taking, have the ability to do it, and preferably have definite long-term goals as regards vocation and eventual work in life (Ch. 1). Interest, ability and purpose result in a strong desire and intention to learn.

Motives

Motives are among the strongest influences on performance. A motive is any factor which determines the amount of effort which you put into a task. Motives derive their strength and driving force from the general fund of energy at your disposal, but the direction of activity is determined by your goals, aspirations and values. That is, motives vary in both strength and direction, and can be considered as vectors.

Effort, as seen from the inside, seems to depend on "will-power" or resolution. Unfortunately merely resolving to work harder is usually ineffective. You can usually do more to improve your work output by changing those features of your environment which are interfering with your work than by making good resolutions to work more. Although it is not

38

easy to control the strength and direction of your motives there are some possible lines of action:

(1) Clarify your vocational aims, get firsthand experience of your chosen vocation, and apply the facts that you learn to practical situations.
(2) Eliminate sources of distraction from the physical environment, and control your attention.
(3) Set yourself definite goals and "deadlines", think of the future, and lengthen your time perspective.
(4) If you can, regularly obtain information about your progress, and find out exactly the nature of your errors and omissions.
(5) Read the history of your subject, learn something of the methods of work of eminent men, and think about the social impact of the disciplines that you study.

The first line of action has already been discussed in Chapter 1. The second involves the control of attention.

The Control of Attention

Concentration is not a "faculty" of the mind, but depends on the control of attention. At any one moment, information is being fed into the brain through all our sensory channels, but usually we are only aware of a small part of it, such as a certain shape or sound. Other bodily sensations do not enter consciousness. In study we have to attend to the verbal and other symbols before us, and their associated meanings and thought-processes, and to neglect all the irrelevant noises, etc., that are going on at the same time. Novel, intense, and sudden stimuli tend to force themselves on our attention. Hence, the working environment should not include novel, intense, and sudden stimuli. Note how difficult it is to sit down and work in a strange place, how distracting loud discontinuous noise is, or any stimulus which appeals to strong interests—such as favorite music, or a conversation on some subject on which we regard ourselves as experts. It is only sense, then, to try and make the working environment contain as few distracting stimuli as possible. These distracting stimuli can include not only noises, conversations, television, etc., but also those arising in ourselves, as feelings of hunger or thirst or pain and discomfort. Much can be done to control all these sources of distraction by controlling our physical surroundings: having a quiet, habitual place for study (Ch. 12).

Usually any particular stimulus is attended to for less than a second. Even if you consciously try to hold an idea in the focus of attention you will not be able to do so for more than a few seconds before some other idea breaks in. Because attention is constantly fluctuating in this fashion, it inevitably wanders off to irrelevant things when we are working slowly and without much purpose. One remedy for inattention, then, is rapid work. Many authors have found, for example, that if they lay a watch by their side, and force themselves to write a page every fifteen minutes, the very speed of the work cures any tendency to "wool-gathering". Moreover, work done against firm time limits is by no means always the least effective. Try and accustom yourself, therefore, to working as rapidly as you reasonably can. This is a sure cure for daydreaming.

Everyone, at times, has trouble in getting down to work. Sometimes it is hard to make a start, as though a certain inertia has to be overcome. Once a start has been made, however, work is often self-sustaining, and exerts a traction on the worker until the task is completed. In order to get over the initial barrier, students are often advised to keep their books and materials laid out to hand in a familiar place, and to pick up a pen and start writing. This is certainly a less effortful procedure than having to gather the necessary work materials together, at the same time screwing up resolve to working pitch. This is, however, a very simplified account of how concentrated work is done.

First, there must be a motive or driving-force impelling you to undertake and complete the task, and we have seen that the most powerful motives arise from goals and interests rather than from external compulsion. Secondly, sustained effort on a task means freedom from distractions and irrelevant trains of thought.

Difficulty in starting and sustaining work can arise from:

(1) lack of motivation, disinterest or fatigue.
(2) conflict with other activities, desires to be doing something else, or the carry-over and perseveration of prior activities and trains of thought.
(3) various kinds of emotional upsets.

Some advice has already been given about motivation and

more is given below in the sections on goals and aspirations, and knowledge of progress. Here I shall deal with what may be called the technique of suppression. One of the important functions of the brain is the suppression of much of the sensory input. Concentrating on a task means suppressing and not attending to unwanted sensory input, and, more important, suppressing the impulse to other activities. Each day there are a great many things to be done, so that it is often hard to decide which to do first and how to fit in all that has to be done. One powerful argument for having a schedule is that it does away with much of the conflict and indecision about the use of time. But, even with a good schedule, it is not easy to concentrate on the work when you are aware of other tasks to be done, and when these other tasks keep intruding themselves into your thoughts.

Imagine a man settling down to work on a summer's morning. He thinks first that the strawberries in the garden will have to be netted soon against the birds, that the engine of his car badly needs overhaul, that there are several letters that he ought to write, that there is a scientific paper which he has to finish by the end of the week, that he badly needs a haircut, and that tomorrow is his wedding anniversary. Writing the scientific paper, he decides, is the job he must get on with and he gives this first priority. Thinking about the other problems in order, he makes a note to buy a garden net on his way home that night, decides to call in at a garage on his way home to get an estimate of the cost of repairs to the car; he then decides that the letters can wait until next day and also the haircut, but that he had better sit down after lunch and do something about the wedding anniversary.

Almost everyone has to plan the daily round in this fashion. Systematic people usually list the things they have to do, decide what is possible, and make a note to carry out later what they cannot do at once. The point is that having made a note and decided on future action, you can then dismiss the matter from your mind and get immersed in the main task. Politicians, and others who handle a large volume of business, often commence their day with a period of quiet planning and meditation. Such planning is even more necessary in study because the work is often difficult, and best tackled in uninterrupted work periods of about some hours' duration. The best work can only be done when you have the right "mental set" and have rekindled the appropriate system of ideas.

If you know that there are certain activities which tend to start trains of thought that interfere with study, don't let these activities get started. Conversations and arguments, for instance, may reverberate in some people's heads for hours afterwards, and prevent them from getting on with their set work. This is true of any prior activity that is uncompleted, leaving the participant in a state of tension.

Even more disturbing are the distractions arising from emotional conflicts and inner disturbances. All that needs to be said here is that you should face up to any personal difficulties, and try to solve them. If you cannot do much to alleviate them, try to accept what cannot be changed.

Goals and Aspirations

Effort is closely related to goals and aspirations. Aspiration is a function of:

(1) your past experience of successes and failures.
(2) your estimate of your chances of success.

The experience of success makes people aim high. If, on the other hand, they think that certain levels of performance are beyond them, they tend to lower their sights.

If a task is too easy or too difficult it presents no challenge; our aspirations are not involved in tasks which are too easy or too difficult. No one experiences feelings of success in performing a very easy task, or feelings of failure when unable to perform one which is much too difficult. For example, an athlete may learn that he can, if he tries hard, run a mile in five minutes. He would have no sense of achievement in running a mile in seven or eight minutes, nor would he aspire to run it in four minutes, as such a time would clearly be beyond his capacity. There is an intermediate zone of difficulty in any task which represents the zone of the individual's capacity, and unless he is very unrealistic his level of aspiration will lie in this zone. Since goal-getting involves a realistic appraisal of your past and likely future performances, it clearly becomes of the greatest importance that you should have accurate information about your performance, in order to set yourself goals to aim at.

Performance is not judged in isolation from that of others. Normally a "good" or "bad" performance is good or bad in relation to the performance of others. Usually the standard of comparison or "reference scale" is set by your status equals, that is by other students on the course. Aspirations are a function of how you perceive your position on a reference scale, and the forces that act on you in that position. For example, the reference scale of a schoolboy in assessing his marks will usually be set by his rank in the class and by the relation of his marks to the marks of others in his class. A champion sheep-shearer or an efficient stenographer will take as reference scales the known rates of work or output of other sheep-shearers or stenographers.

The forces acting on the individual in his perceived position in the reference scale will depend on the "social climate". Very often in schools and elsewhere this climate is competitive, so that the individual is under constant pressure to improve his score in relation to that of others. In other cases performance much above the mean of others may be regarded as socially undesirable, as sometimes happens among industrial workers on piece work, or in schools and universities where it is "bad form" to work too hard. Here there may be definite social pressures on the more productive workers to slow down their rate of work.

From much experimental work on aspirations it can be said that:

(1) Where success is defined as attaining a self-set goal, success usually leads to raising aspirations.
(2) Shifts in aspiration reflect changes in the subject's confidence in his ability to attain his goals.
(3) The effects of failure are more variable than the effects of success. Repeated failure often causes the individual to give up trying altogether. This occurs when the highest level of performance of which he is capable lags so badly behind that of others, or occupies such a low place on his reference scale, that it has no value for him. If on the other hand he wants very much to succeed, and believes that he can, failure may cause him to redouble his efforts.

Most people are realistic and tie their aspirations very closely to the level of their past performance. Usually it is placed a little higher than the level previously attained, and thus provides a spur to effort, but not too great a disappointment if failure results. Psychologists usually think that those who set their aspirations at absurdly high levels would do better to be more realistic. The goals that you set yourself should be goals that you can, with effort, reasonably expect to attain.

Knowledge of Results

In the course of learning it is helpful to have some measure of your progress, at regular intervals. If you have a weekly test or examination, for instance, you can chart your progress, and compete against yourself, by constantly trying to improve on your last performance. In most colleges, however, regular assessments of work are not made, so that students have some difficulty in knowing whether they are doing enough work or not, and whether they are on the right lines in what they are doing.

Many experiments show the advantages of obtaining immediate and precise information about the outcome of your efforts. (One of the reasons why the new teaching machines are successful is that they give the learner immediate information about the nature of his successes and failures.)

A simple way to demonstrate the importance of knowledge of results is to get two subjects to draw straight lines freehand, with instructions to make them three inches long. Each line should be covered up as it is drawn so that it cannot serve as a copy for the next. Give one subject no information about the accuracy of his performance, and he will not improve. Give the other subject exact information about each line that he draws, telling him by how much it is too short or too long. After a few tries he will be able to draw a three-inch line very accurately. Many other experiments yield essentially similar results. In order to improve the learner needs to know whether his responses are correct or not.

The graph on page 45 shows the average number of additions performed in a minute by a group who were allowed to count up how many addition examples they had completed after each trial, compared with the performance of a group who did not know what their score was.

The importance of "feedback" to the learner of the results of his efforts is most obvious in learning of physical skills. Much skill learning is of course self-correcting, in the sense that the learner knows at once whether he has made an adequate response or not. In piano-playing, for example, there is auditory feedback; in typing the typed paper record gives immediate visual information about errors. In many games, however, such as swimming, tennis, or golf, it is much more difficult for the learner to get a clear idea of the results of his efforts. Hence the need for coaches and instructors. In skilled performances, such as shooting at a distant target, if no knowledge of results is given to the learner, no improvement is possible. Whatever can be done to help the learner to assess his own efforts is helpful. Practice before a mirror is useful for dancing and golf. Athletes are helped by slow-motion photography of their action. Graphic recordings of the

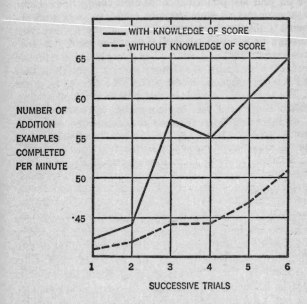

Fig. 5. *The influence of knowledge of score on performance*

foot movements made in a skilled industrial process helped trainees to master the skill.

Interest and motivation in a task are enhanced when the worker can see the results of his efforts. In mowing a lawn, or in writing an essay, for example, he can look proudly back on the visible results of his efforts.

In study, motivation sometimes flags because no quantitative measure of progress is available. At school the final grades, however unreliable, provide some tangible evidence of performance. At college the student often has to learn to appraise and regulate his own progress.

Extending Your Knowledge

Finally a good way of generating interest in your work is to read widely, to study its history and methods, its social impact on society, and its relation to other similar disciplines. The more you learn about a subject the easier it becomes. This point needs stressing because there are some students, with peculiar ideas of brain physiology, who think they must not overtax their memories with facts. They think that each fact "occupies" one brain cell, and as they only have a limited number of brain cells, they must restrict themselves to a limited number of facts. Nothing could be further from the truth. Facts are not stored in this simple mechanical way. The brain is rather a vast interconnecting network, and the more complex and interconnected it becomes the more efficiently it works. Most people of fertile intelligence read widely, and get fresh insights into their particular subjects by the constant effort to encompass new sets of facts.

Changing Habits

If you mean to work to a plan and to become a more effective worker, you will have to change some of your habits, possibly some habits of long standing. This is the most difficult step of all. Nearly everyone realizes that he could work a lot more effectively, but is unable to bring about the requisite changes in behavior. It is not easy to change long-standing habits, but behavior does change with changes in the environment. Think of the changes that take place on vacation in a foreign country, on marriage, in a new job, on being drafted into the armed forces, on leaving home and becoming independent of parents. Clearly even if you believe that you cannot change your ways by an effort of will, you can change them by altering your environment, over which you have at least some control. Further, if you can trace back any behavior to its cause you may well be able to alter it.

If you have difficulty in studying, reflect on the cause. Try and list your difficulties. It may be all or any of these things:

(1) *In the work itself and your relation to it.*

Disinterest and boredom—you can't see the use of the subject, or relate it to your purposes.

Difficulty of the subject—possibly you lack a groundwork in the subject which is taken for granted—or you really have no aptitude for the subject.

Fear of failure—a fear that whatever efforts you make they will not be successful.

The work takes you too long—you become tired and listless, and make no progress.

Lack of the necessary books and materials.

(2) *Conflict with other activities.*

Desire to be doing something other than studying.

Invitations from friends, and interruptions.

Taking on too many extra-curricular activities.

(3) *Distractions in the immediate environment.*

Noises, music, television.

Room too hot or too cold.

Sofas or easy chairs—inviting somnolence.

(4) *Worry about personal affairs.*

Having made your analysis, consider what remedial action needs to be taken, and work out in detail how you propose to change your habits.

Habit Formation

Each person has a great many habit systems, which, when activated by a motive, come into play in familiar situations. For example, when confronted by a difficult intellectual problem some people may habitually shut themselves up and puzzle over it alone, some may habitually go to another person for assistance, and some may habitually give up and convince themselves that the problem is of no importance. In each case the habit system arises and gains its strength because it has in the past led to success or satisfaction or to the resolution of the difficulty. Habit systems are fixated and reinforced when they lead to success, relief from tension, etc.

In the simplest case, the acquisition of a conditioned response, the strength of the habit is a positive growth function of the number of previous occasions on which the habit has been performed, and has led to satisfying consequences. The general rule, then, is that habits are fixed by the consequences that they lead to. Actions which lead to satisfying consequences are repeated and become habitual; actions which lead to failure or to dissatisfaction are dropped.

This rule underlines the need for early success: the new habit which you are trying to establish should lead fairly soon to satisfaction of some kind. The satisfaction may be of many kinds—self-satisfaction because work has been well done, praise from others, or even some small material indulgence, self-administered, as a reward. Habits of regular work tend to bring their own reward, in the shape of feelings of

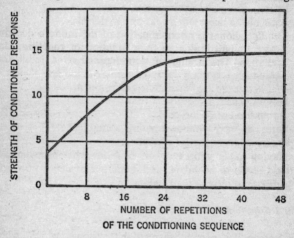

Fig. 6. Strength of a conditioned response during the course of conditioning

conscious virtue or in a sense of attainment, but external rewards are also useful in keeping the new habit going in its early stages.

Habit Formation and Change

What are the best ways of breaking undesirable habits and forming good ones? For advice on this topic we still have to turn to writers of the last century. Before Darwin's day, habit was regarded as all-powerful. Nineteenth-century moralists earnestly advised young people to develop habits of sobriety, industry and perseverance. Cobbett, for example, advised young men who wished to master English grammar to acquire the habit of perseverance.

"When you find weariness approaching, rouse yourself, and remember, that, if you give up, all that you have done has been done in vain. . . . If reason interfere and bid you *overcome the fits of lassitude,* and almost mechanically to go on without the stimulus of hope, the buoyant fit speedily returns; you congratulate yourself that you did not yield to the temptation to abandon your pursuit, and you proceed with more vigor than ever. Five or six triumphs over temptation to indolence or despair lay the foundation of certain success; and what is of still more importance, fix in you the *habit of perseverance.*"

Cobbett's account is an anticipation of the modern doctrine that habit strength builds up as a function of repetition and reinforcement. The notion of perseverance as a habit that can be acquired is supported by modern theories of conditioning and learning.

Nowadays people are, however, somewhat skeptical of schemes for self-improvement. But the advice of the older writers is still worth looking at. The Scottish philosopher Bain (1859) saw morals and habits of regular work as opposed to appetites and indulgences. In childhood and youth there is inevitably conflict between desires and moral behavior, but, with proper training, desires are overcome with less and less effort, until the well-trained adult feels no temptations. Appetites are only tamed, however, by long habit backed by some kind of compulsion or by the good example of others. Habits running counter to strong appetites can only be set up if we launch ourselves on a new course of action with a strong initiative and never allow any backslidings to occur. The strongest motive is external compulsion; next comes the example and persuasion of others; the weakest motive is our own determination and "willpower".

Take the practice of regular early rising. Many industrial workers rise at 6 a.m. with mechanical punctuality and entire indifference, because since early youth they have had to be out of bed each morning at six o'clock to go to work. With them, external compulsion and an unbroken series of early risings enable them to rise early without effort.

Three Maxims

Following up Bain's account, William James (1890) formulated three oft-quoted maxims:

"The first maxim is that in the acquisition of a new habit,

or the leaving off of an old one, we must take care to launch ourselves with as strong and decided an initiative as possible. Accumulate all the possible circumstances which shall re-enforce the new way; make engagements incompatible with the old; take a public pledge, if the case allows; in short, envelope your resolution with every aid you know. . . .

"The second maxim is: Never suffer an exception to occur till the new habit is securely rooted in your life. Each lapse is like the letting fall of a ball of string which one is carefully winding up; a single slip undoes more than a great many turns will wind again. . . .

"The need for securing success at the outset is imperative. Failure at first is apt to damp the energy of all future attempts, whereas past experiences of success nerve one to future vigor. . . .

"The question of 'tapering-off' in abandoning such habits as drink and opium-indulgence comes in here, and is a question about which experts differ within certain limits, and in regard to what may be best for the individual case. In the main, however, all expert opinion would agree that abrupt acquisition of the new habit is the best way, if there be a real possibility of carrying it out . . . provided one can stand it, a sharp period of suffering, and then a free time, is the best thing to aim at, whether in giving up a habit like that of opium, or in simply changing one's hours of rising or of work. It is surprising how soon a desire will die of inanition if it is never fed.

"A third maxim may be added to the preceding pair: Seize the very first possible opportunity to act on every resolution you make, and on every emotional prompting you may experience in the direction of the habits you aspire to gain. It is not the moment of their forming, but in the moment of their producing motor effects, that resolves and aspirations communicate a new 'set' to the brain. . . .

"No matter how full a reservoir of maxims one may possess, and no matter how good one's sentiments may be, if one has not taken advantage of every concrete opportunity to act, one's character may remain entirely unaffected for the better. With mere good intentions, hell is proverbially paved."

In general James's advice is still good today. If you want to change your habits, make a clean break with the old behavior. If periods of indulgence are admitted to break into the career of the learner, effortless performance of the desired change will never be attained.

An example of an organization which puts many of these maxims into practice is Alcoholics Anonymous. This movement has had some striking successes in reclaiming alcoholics when all other methods have failed. The sufferer signs the pledge—there is a sharp break with former habits. He makes a public pledge of his intentions. He meets fellow-sufferers who are in process of conquering their addiction. Members of the society give each other support and advice, and reinforce each other's purpose and resolution. The organization also provides other activities, such as meetings where nonalcoholic drinks are supplied, which can replace the dependence on alcohol. Your task in setting up desirable habits of work is, of course, very different from overcoming a physiological addiction. But the same general principles apply both to setting up new habits and to changing old ones.

The Power of Group Decision

Strength can be given to your determination if you can enter into a compact with friends to do more work or to work more systematically. The force of group decision is greater than the force of individual decision—it is more likely to lead to action. Reading a book or going to a lecture on how to study may set up in you the right intentions. Intentions alone, however, if they rely on individual "willpower", are often not sufficient to lead to change. The link between intention and action can often be provided by group decision. Group decision is effective because of "commitment" to friends and other members of the group.

Summary

Merely resolving to work harder is usually ineffective. But you can enhance your motivation by setting yourself both short-term and long-term goals, by controlling sources of distraction, by charting your progress, and by immersing yourself in your studies.

Rapid work is one cure for difficulty in concentrating. Another aid is the technique of suppression. Since unwillingness to settle down to study is often the result of a wish to be doing something else, you need to suppress the impulse to other activities. This is best achieved by allocating a sensible amount of time to other intruding tasks and activities, and having made a plan, dismissing them from consciousness.

CHAPTER FOUR

LEARNING AND REMEMBERING

Small have continuous plodders ever won
Save base authority from others' books.
                                    SHAKESPEARE

The Course of Learning

MOST subjects of study are too complex to yield a curve of
learning in which a quantitative measure of progress is
plotted against the amount of practice. But such curves can
readily be derived for physical skills such as typewriting. If
we plot the number of strokes that can be made per minute
against the amount of practice, we get a curve of learning.
One such curve might be:

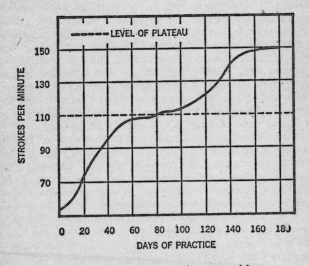

Fig. 7. Learning curve for typewriting

Notice (1) the initial period of very little progress, as the learner finds his way about the task. If you take up an entirely new subject there is bound to be a period of small progress, as you learn to deal with new concepts and a new technical vocabulary; (2) a period of rapid progress as you begin to "see the light" and are spurred on by the interest and novelty of the task; (3) a "plateau" or period of slow progress, as a result of flagging interest and the increased difficulty of the task; and finally (4) a slower climb to the upper limit of skill.

Not all learning curves of course will be of this form and there will be irregularities and short-term fluctuations in the individual case. The important point to note is that learning takes time, and that there are often periods of little obvious progress. The moral is not to become discouraged when you seem to be stuck on a "plateau". As you accumulate experience difficulties often seem to disappear. In all learning, advances tend to come irregularly and in bursts, as you gain fresh insights into the subject.

The Importance of Understanding

In order to obtain these insights you must thoroughly understand what you are studying. If you really understand a subject not only do you remember it easily, but you can apply your knowledge in new situations. The important thing is not what you know, but what you can do with what you know. The extra effort involved in getting a firm grounding in the essentials of a subject is repaid many times in later study.

How are you to achieve understanding? Understanding involves (1) linking new knowledge to the old and (2) organizing it and remembering it in a systematic fashion.

To retain and make sense of any new concept or fact it must be linked in as many ways as possible to your existing body of knowledge. All good introductory textbooks are constantly giving familiar examples, or using analogies, or appealing to common experience. In setting out the differences between daylight vision and twilight vision, for example, most writers point out that as twilight falls in the garden, blue flowers remain blue for some time after red blossoms appear black, illustrating, by appeal to common experience, that under dim illumination the colors of the blue end of the spectrum become relatively brighter than those of the red end. Or again, to illustrate that the movement of any particular electron during the passage of an electric current is only a few centimeters per second, although the velocity of the current is extremely great, the analogy is often used of a boxcar run into the end of a long line of boxcars in a freight yard, a corresponding boxcar being rapidly ejected from the far end. Linking new information to familiar experience in this fashion always helps understanding.

In order to tie the new information to your stock of knowledge with as many links as possible, you must reflect on it, and try and relate it to what you already know. Thinking the matter over by yourself, writing out summaries of the main points, and talking to other students about it, are all valuable for fixing it more clearly in your mind.

In the words of William James: "The more other facts a fact is associated with in the mind, the better possession of it our memory retains. Each of its associates becomes a hook to which it hangs, a means to fish it up by when sunk beneath the surface. . . . Of two men with the same outward experiences and the same amount of mere natural tenacity, the one who *thinks* over his experiences most, and weaves them into systematic relations with each other, will be the one with the best memory. . . . The college athlete who remains a dunce at his books will astonish you by his knowledge of men's 'records' in various feats and games, and will be a walking dictionary of sporting statistics. The reason is that he is constantly going over these things in his mind, and comparing and making series of them."

A System of Study: SQ3R

An aid to systematic study which has proved of value in colleges and universities is the system called SQ3R.* The SQ3R stands for:

Survey
Question
Read
Recite
Review

(1) *Survey*. In brief, this means that instead of picking

* F. P. Robinson. *Effective Study*. New York: Harper and Row, 1961.

up a textbook and reading one of its chapters over and over, you should first "survey": that is, find out all you can about the aims and purpose of the book, read the author's preface, study the table of contents and the index, read the chapter summaries (if there are summaries) and skim your way rapidly through the book. Keep in mind your own purpose in study, the syllabus you are trying to cover, and the relevance of the book to your own special interests. And if the book does not suit your purpose, if it is not well written, and at the right level of difficulty, search around until you find a better one. In other words, make a reconnaissance before you start your main work, and get an overall perspective of what lies before you.

(2) *Question.* The second preparatory step—asking questions—is also important. This entails going rapidly through the chapters of the book which you are going to tackle, and jotting down such questions as occur to you. This is useful because it motivates you and gives you a purpose: it forces you to think and to marshal such knowledge as you already have. Many good authors help the reader by clearly stating a problem in their introductory sentences or specifically confronting the reader with questions. And if you persist in maintaining a questioning attitude, you will in time come to read books critically: you will ask what evidence the author has for his statements and whether what he is saying is consistent with what you already know or believe. No intelligent person merely reads a book. He cannot help dwelling on particular points as he reads, and contrasting or uniting them with other points that he has just grasped.

(3) *Reading.* Next comes reading proper. The first reading of a textbook chapter usually needs to be rather slow and thorough. If you are a voracious reader of novels or detective stories you must not carry over to textbooks your habit of rapid reading for entertainment. Most good textbook chapters have a structure of headings and subheadings which you need to keep in the back of your mind as you read. Often you must turn back to previous pages to remind yourself of some fact or argument. If the subject is illustrated by graphs or by diagrams, you will often be well advised to copy them out or elaborate them. Complex arguments and masses of information can often be presented briefly and neatly in a table or graph. Hence, if you are foolish enough to skip the graphs or tables you will often miss the major points that the author is trying to make. More-

over, most people will find, if they will take the trouble to master them, that graphs and diagrams are much more easily remembered than long verbal statements, and serve as convenient foundations around which to build a structure of knowledge.

(4) *Recitation.* A single reading is never enough, even though you read actively with intent to remember. The next stage in study is therefore recitation. Bacon said: "If you read anything over twenty times you will not learn it by heart so easily as if you were to read it only ten, trying to repeat it between whiles, and when memory failed looking at the book."

Recitation is certainly an old-fashioned method, and to many it suggests classes in elementary school—learning off, parrot-fashion, the multiplication table or some lines of verse. The last thing we want is that our learning should be rote and meaningless.

By recitation is meant here not word-for-word repetition, or learning by heart, but outlining the substance of a passage. The outline provides the framework into which more details can be fitted in subsequent recitation.

Literal word-for-word recitation is only applicable when formulas or foreign language vocabularies or anatomical facts have to be memorized, and, on such materials, it is of advantage to use about three-quarters of the available time in recitation. But nothing should ever be learnt as an isolated, meaningless unit. Formulas can be derived from first principles, foreign language words can be understood by studying their roots and derivations, and anatomical facts can be memorized better by starting with simplified diagrams to which detail is added. Sometimes, however, things have to be taken as given and they have to be committed to memory. Then recitation is of great help. With more meaningful material, recitation must not degenerate into rote learning and become a substitute for thought; and it may be of little use in the early stages of learning.

So recitation is of most value in learning those things which have to be got off by heart, such as the multiplication table and the alphabet; but it is still good practice, after reading each major section of a chapter, to lay the book on one side and try and recall what you have been reading. This simple procedure is often revealing. Sometimes you can recall very little and must conclude that your learning is in a very immature stage. More frequently you will realize that there

are some specific gaps in your knowledge which you must go
back and fill in. Certainly the procedure cures that habit,
often a relic of school days, of thinking that because you have
read through a chapter, you have "done it" and know it. In
my experience, four or five readings and recitations are usually required before textbook materials of average difficulty can
be mastered. Repetition of itself is of no value, but each
repetition, if you are reading actively and alertly, should
add to your insight into the material.

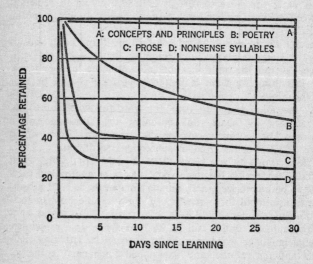

Fig. 8. Curves of forgetting for different types of material

(5) *Reviewing.* The final step of SQ3R is Reviewing. Reviewing should not be regarded as something to be undertaken just before examinations. One of the most practical
results of memory experiments is that material that has to be
retained over long periods should be studied and restudied.
Memories become stronger and stronger with each relearning, and forgetting proceeds more slowly. Let us examine the
curve of forgetting. Material into which there is real insight
is not forgotten. For all other materials forgetting is at first
very rapid and then becomes slower.

The permanence of your learning should be of concern to
you. Ask yourself how much you can remember of your
school Latin or geometry or French, and you will probably

find that unless you have been recently using or practicing a subject, the greater part of it will have been forgotten. Research studies (see graph) suggest that typically, after two years, the average student scores only about 30 per cent of the perfect score on a test of factual knowledge. General principles and general understandings, on the other hand, are retained for much longer.

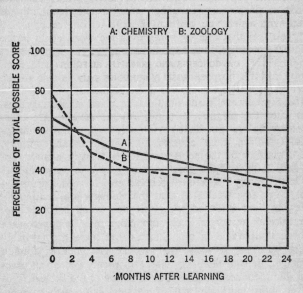

Fig. 9. Recall scores for college subjects

Common experience suggests that the details of what we learn fade very quickly, often within the first hour or so. Indeed, in listening to an hour's lecture much of the early part of the lecture may have been forgotten well before the end— so that experienced teachers repeat and recapitulate the important points of their lectures at the end. To prevent the sudden and catastrophic loss which takes place so early, early reviewing is required. That means going over the lecture or piece of work again as soon as possible afterwards, thinking about it, or discussing it with others or applying the facts and knowledge in some practical exercise. You should certainly go over your notes of lectures, work periods and experiments the very same day—even if it is only for a few minutes.

This practical advice is seldom carried out, I fancy, because, having taken down some written record, you have misplaced confidence that you will be able to recreate the original at any future date. Alas! this seldom turns out to be true. As the time of examination draws near only too often you will not be able to make head or tail of those lecture notes which you took down six months ago and have not looked at since—nor remember some crucial detail of that experiment which you omitted to write up on the day.

If you feel that merely going over the work again is too tedious an exercise, read another account of the same subject in a textbook, expanding your notes by additions and comments: for this purpose write your notes on one side of the paper only, to leave room for these additions.

The first review, then, should take place as soon as possible after the original learning. Further reviews are often necessary before the final review which precedes examinations. Consider those courses, like medicine and surgery, where mastery of the subject matter is literally a matter of life and death, and the pass mark may have to be set at 100 per cent. Nearly all medical schools give tests and examinations every few weeks, so that the students are continually reviewing their knowledge. In this way recall becomes mechanical and automatic. Such automation may be unnecessary or even undesirable in arts subjects, but there are probably aspects of most subjects, such as the grammar of foreign languages, or statistical formulas, which can well be so practiced that their use becomes second nature to the subject. This is even more markedly true of physical skills such as typewriting or driving a car or swimming or hitting a golf ball, where the essence of skilled performance consists of reducing the skill to an automatic level. We take it for granted that physical skills develop gradually and demand repeated practice for their perfection. The same is true of some aspects of study.

In review before examinations you should pay particular attention to the earlier material you have learnt, as more of it will have been forgotten. You should leave yourself time to go over all the material you have covered. Studies have shown that subjective estimates of strengths and weaknesses are often at fault. You are often weak on material which you are confident you know well. Active reviewing, and a few attempts at answering old examination questions should give you a better idea of where your true strengths and weaknesses lie.

You will realize that the amount of time that you give to each of the steps of the SQ3R study technique will depend on the subjects you are studying. The natural sciences, the social sciences, the arts, and practical and vocational subjects differ in their aims and methods. The wide and discursive reading which is expected of students of English literature, for example, is not required in an applied science, where there is a basic core of facts and techniques which must be mastered before elementary competence can be reached. The SQ3R method can, however, be applied in principle to all fields of study. It is very like the famous steps of instruction of the nineteenth-century German educationist, Herbart: preparation, presentation, association, generalization and application. Preparation includes our first two steps of survey and question, in which the aims of study are set out, and the learner is encouraged to marshal his present stock of knowledge. Presentation and association include the reading and recitation stages, rather more stress being put by Herbart on thinking and reflection than on sheer recitation as a means of uniting the new knowledge with the old. Herbart's final steps of generalization, that is, the drawing of general truths and principles, and the application of knowledge to practice, need to be added to the SQ3R formula. If you are concerned, as you should be, not only to pass examinations, but to retain your knowledge for a working lifetime, and to put it to good use, you must attempt to reduce it to general principles, and to apply it in practice.

Rote Learning and Insightful Learning

To emphasize once again that your learning must be meaningful, let us consider the difference between rote learning and insightful learning. Rote learning means learning isolated and meaningless bits of knowledge. Insightful learning means organizing your knowledge into meaningful units. Grouping materials according to a principle helps both learning and memory. In order to demonstrate the value of principles, the following numbers were presented to groups of students:

$$2\ 9\ 3\ 3\ 3\ 6\ 4\ 0\ 4\ 3\ 4\ 7$$
$$5\ 8\ 1\ 2\ 1\ 5\ 1\ 9\ 2\ 2\ 2\ 6$$

One group was given three minutes to discover the principle involved. Other groups spent the same time in memorizing the figures. After three weeks 23 per cent of the principle-seekers could still reproduce the figures correctly, but none of the memorizers could.

See if you can find the principle on which the two rows of figures are constructed.

Why are principles better retained than material learned by rote? Usually because when a principle has been discovered there is far less to remember. In this example the principle-seekers only had to remember the first figures in each line (29 and 5) and how the series was constructed (by adding alternately 3 and 4). Instead of having to remember 24 separate digits they had only to remember 3 items.

This example should bring home to you the great economy of learning general rules and principles rather than a mass of facts.

To convince yourself still further that meaningful material can be learned and retained much more easily than disconnected matter, such as nonsense syllables or lists of unrelated words, try the following experiment. Read the list of 12 nonsense syllables below three times, with the intention of reproducing them in order. Then close the book and see how many you can write down.

bep, tev, wib, kuj, jid, paf, seb, zih, fiw, nuy, leb, ruw.

Next, read the 12 words below three times, trying to memorize the words in order and then try to reproduce them:

house, field, brook, bridge, fish, swim, duck, water, drink, cup, saucer, plate.

You will have much more success with the word list than with the nonsense list, partly because of familiarity with common words, and partly because the words present a sequence of ideas, or chain of associations, which facilitates memorizing. If you go over the word list and organize it by making up a story which includes the words in order, retention will be better still. From the principle illustrated in this little experiment it follows that you should fit items to be remembered into a system of ideas. Often making a chart or diagram or table will help.

Organizing and Memorizing

Actively organizing what we learn has another advantage.
The form in which material is learned partly determines the
form in which it will be recalled. There are three processes
in learning and remembering: (1) original learning or im-
printing, (2) storage, (3) retrieval. Often the difficulty in remembering seems to be not so much in storing information
as in retrieving it just when we want it. This usually means
that it has been stored away poorly or untidily. An analogy
is helpful here. Think of your memory as a large storehouse
containing many storage shelves, situated on a multitude of
interconnecting paths. Information is fed into the store, and
the storeman has the job of storing it away in labelled jars
and containers on appropriate shelves. Much of the incoming
information the storeman rejects as worthless or very unlikely to be needed, and either he doesn't take it in at all or
else stores it away in some dim inner recess. The incoming
information which seems to him useful and important and
likely to be required again soon, he stores in some handy ac-
cessible shelf. Moreover, a good storeman doesn't store information away in a random fashion. His shelves and containers are classified and labelled, and new items are filed
away systematically in the class to which they belong, and
near other similar materials. Then when the owner of the
storehouse is faced with a problem which may be anything
from choosing a summer vacation, mixing cement, solving a
mathematical equation or writing an examination answer, the
relevant information comes to hand: the person has a good
memory.

The analogy must not be pressed too far, of course. No
one knows how the brain stores information, but it is probably an electro-chemical process rather than a mechanical
one. The point of the analogy is to bring home to you that
recall is much better when learned materials are committed
to the memory store in an orderly and structured fashion. If
you have filed away your facts carelessly, you may not be
able to retrieve them when you want them. Often, in discussing examination papers, students insist that they knew
the answer to the question but did not realize what sort of
answer was required; or the wording of the question was
such that it did not connect with their store of information.
When this happens it usually means that they have failed to
organize their learning materials, have tried to memorize

isolated facts, failed to think, or failed to achieve the right grasp of the materials at the outset.

How can you best organize your materials? For the purpose of passing written examinations the most efficient procedure is to file your facts away in the form in which you will need them. Teachers who are determined to get as many pupils as they can through their examinations often give them systematic notes—such as: What were the causes of the French Revolution?

(1) The existing system of government.
(2) Influence of the philosophers.
(3) Example of American Revolution.
(4) Character of Louis and Marie Antoinette.
(5) Bankruptcy of government.
(6) Famine, cold and mobs.

Then, providing that the pupil can memorize these six points about the causes of the French Revolution, he is in a good position to write an acceptable answer on that topic. Such summaries are useful because they enable large quantities of information to be stored in systematic form. The list of points can serve as a framework around which a full knowledge of the subject can be acquired. Similarly in taking notes, it is good practice to number or letter your major headings and subdivide the major paragraphs: 1 (a), (b), (c) or A(i), (ii), (iii). All such devices are helpful, provided that the structure suits the material and provided that the material is not learnt in parrot-fashion. The danger of such mnemonic devices is that they do lend themselves to "spoon-feeding", and to the mechanical reproduction of material without much understanding. They can become substitutes for thought, effort and understanding. It is far better for you to impose your own structure on the material than to take over the structure which someone else has imposed on it. If you take over the structure from your personal teacher, he will be able to expand and build on the structure he has set before you. But structures taken over from the various "study-guides" and cribs which purport to summarize the essentials of a subject are usually worthless, and purchased mainly by those who have neglected their studies to such an extent that they fall back in desperation on this potted information.

Memory and Memory Systems

Almost everyone would like to be able to improve his memory. Unfortunately no one can improve his general retentiveness—memory is not an entity like a muscle that can be improved by exercise. But you can certainly improve ways of remembering particular subjects. Former generations of schoolboys had to learn large portions of *Paradise Lost* or the *Iliad* in order to improve the "faculty" of memory. The fallacy of this "memory-training" was demonstrated by William James. He and his students memorized a poem by Hugo, timing themselves to see how long the learning took. They then "exercised" their memories by learning other poems every day for a month. Finally they timed themselves as they memorized a new poem by Hugo. The improvement resulting from all this practice was so small that James concluded that no amount of training would improve general retentiveness. The way to improve memory is to learn more about the subject matter and to try and understand it better.

Ability to memorize can be improved, not by lengthy practice in memorizing, but by learning better methods of remembering. These methods have been found useful:

(1) Use of active self-testing or recitation.
(2) Use of grouping and rhythm (the multiplication table is often taught in a kind of sing-song).
(3) Attention to meaning and the use of associations (developing as many associations as possible).
(4) Alertness and concentration (a strong intention to learn).

There are a number of memory systems, out of which quacks and pseudo-psychologists still make a living, which claim to improve memory. They mostly depend on developing ingenious and artificial associations between otherwise disconnected facts.

You can learn the value of π to the 13th decimal place by memorizing:

> How I wish I could determine
> of circle round
> the exact relation
> Archimedes found.

Put down the number of letters in each word and you have

$$=3.1415926535895$$

A commonly used device is the "figure-alphabet" for remembering dates and numbers. The numbers are translated into letters which are then combined in some word. The word is more easily remembered. For example, the following figure alphabet (which omits vowels) may be used:

1	2	3	4	5	6	7	8	9	0
t	n	m	r	l	sh	g	f	b	s
d					j	k	v	p	c
					ch	c			z
					g	qu			

First the figure alphabet must be memorized. Then to remember that your friend lives at house number 947, b r and g are the letters required. A vowel is included to make a word such as brag, and you can then "brag" that you can remember your friend's number.

Feats of memory can also be performed by learning:

> one is a bun
> two is a shoe
> three is a tree
> four is a door
> five is a hive
> six are sticks
> seven is heaven
> eight is a gate
> nine is a line, and
> ten is a hen

Then to remember a series of ten objects or events in order you form an association between each and the appropriate word in the above list.

These systems are, however, so artificial that you should be able to do much better by developing real and logical associations yourself. Learning and recall are in fact about 25 per cent better when sensible logical connections between items are developed than when artificial connections are made according to some system. The success of any of the commercial "systems" results more from the stimulus that they give to the learner's efforts than from any other cause. Any intelligent person can do better on his own, provided he gives his attention to the task. Usually it is easy to find an intermediate idea or association which will link two ideas together.

Overlearning

Let us look at learning from another aspect. When you learn something, and remember it, some kind of a memory trace is laid down in the brain. Whether you are able to retain a given fact will depend on two things: (1) the strength of the memory trace—which will depend on how thorough your learning has been, and (2) the strength of interfering factors which work to destroy or weaken the trace.

You can increase the strength of your memory traces by overlearning your lessons, taking precautions against subsequent interference, and by distributing your practice over a period of time.

Material is underlearned when it has not been studied long enough for you to be able to recall it 100 per cent correctly. It is overlearned when you continue to practice it after you can recall it 100 per cent correctly. For instance, it might take you 10 minutes to learn a vocabulary of 20 foreign words. If you then carry on learning and reciting with the same close attention as before you are overlearning the material. Another 5 minutes would represent 50 per cent overlearning, another 10 minutes 100 per cent. Overlearning strengthens the memory trace. Things which nearly everyone has overlearned would include the alphabet, the multiplication table and nursery rhymes. We are never likely to forget these as long as we live. Motor skills are also overlearned: you don't forget how to ride a bicycle or to type or swim after a long period of disuse. This suggests that if you want to remember something for a long time, you should overlearn it.

The graph shows you that sheer memorizing of meaningless materials is helped by overlearning. An overlearned list is retained better than one badly learnt, but diminishing returns soon set in, and you will see that the difference between the 50 per cent and 100 per cent curves is less than that between the 50 per cent and 0 per cent curve. The graph should serve to convince you once again of how inefficient rote learning is. Even with 100 per cent overlearning rather less than 10 per cent is retained after 28 days, when there has been no further practice between learning and recall. Certainly your original learning should be

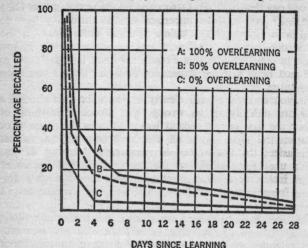

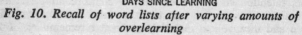

DAYS SINCE LEARNING

Fig. 10. Recall of word lists after varying amounts of overlearning

thorough, but it is more important to organize and understand the material than to go on saying it over to yourself mechanically.

Interference

To deal now with the factors that destroy or weaken the memory trace. It seems to take time for the traces to become consolidated, so that if your learning is followed immediately by some other form of strenuous mental work this will interfere with the retention of the original learning. Very often forgetting occurs when one set of ideas has got mixed up with another. If you begin to learn two similar foreign languages at the same time, for instance, such as Italian and French, you will recall words in one language while trying to speak the other; the French word may "block" the Italian, and vice versa.

This kind of interference is greatest in the early stages of learning, before you completely learn or understand the material, and the more similar the two sets of material the greater will be the interference. It occurs most obviously in spelling foreign words and in mathematics. If you learn on one day that $(2x)$ $(3y) = 6xy$ and on the next day that (X^3) $(X^2) = X^5$ you may be uncertain on the third day how to deal with $(2X^3)$ $(3X^2)$ unless you are quite clear on the distinction between coefficient and an exponent. Or if you learn in one hour that the French for book is "livre" and in the next hour that the Italian for book is "libro", confusion may ensue.

If you can distinguish clearly between the two situations you are unlikely to go wrong; and thorough learning of either the first or the second lesson reduces the chances of interference. Once again all that is known in this subject emphasizes the importance of meaningful learning. If you really understand what you are learning you will not suffer from interference. One important practical rule that follows from this discussion is that in the *early* stages of learning you should make sure that you cover the ground thoroughly, even if this means that progress will seem slow.

If forgetting is caused by interference from new learning, retention should be best if you relax completely after learning, or better still, go to sleep. It is actually true that rote and meaningless materials are better remembered after sleep than after a period awake.

Memory for connected and logical materials is, however, very little affected by the normal sequence of waking activities. So you must not conclude that the time just before you go to sleep is the best time to memorize. You will probably be too tired to concentrate properly, or you will find that an active period of study prior to going to bed will make it hard for you to get to sleep.

Storing Information

We now turn to a fascinating topic—the changes that go on spontaneously in your memory. Consider yourself for a moment as a recording machine. First you receive information (learning). Second you store the information away (memory), and finally you retrieve and reproduce it (recall). This process is by no means mechanical. Much of the information which strikes our sense organs is never even registered, and much is immediately forgotten. It is as well that this is so, otherwise the sheer task of registering and storing information would be colossal. Instead, we usually only notice and remember those things which are relevant to our purposes. From the first, perception is selective. When you are listening to a lecture you are usually not aware of extraneous sights and sounds, but concentrate (or should do!) on what the speaker is saying. Even so, you probably miss a good deal of what is being said, by allowing your attention to lapse or starting off on thought-trails of your own; or you are busy getting some notes down and the lecturer gets ahead of you. So if a hundred people listen to a lecture each will have got a slightly different version of it. The same thing applies to the reading of textbooks. As you read there will be lapses of attention or you will start thinking of something else as your eyes continue to scan the letters. All this is inevitable, and must be allowed for: we have to select from the available mass of information which is constantly stimulating our sense organs. A human being is very quick at taking in familiar material. You can recognize a short sentence in 1/10th of a second. Even so there is a limit to the amount of a complicated sentence that you can take in in a given time.

Once any idea has registered or entered our consciousness, it will be stored much better if we deliberately try to remember it. Again there are limits to the rate at which you can store information. The immediate memory span of even very intelligent adults is limited to about nine digits: that is to say very few people can repeat more than nine digits which have been said over to them at the rate of one per second, as 3–7–1–8–2–6–4–9–5. This means that no one can hold in mind more than about nine disconnected symbols even for a very short time, and even when the symbols are very familiar. A sentence of about twenty words can, however, be repeated in this fashion, showing that, when the items to be remembered make sense and are linked together, memory span is much greater. This should suggest to you that connected meaningful material is easier to store away and remember than meaningless material.

When we consider recall after a time interval, we can see at once that it is not a mechanical process but often a *reconstruction*. Suppose you have a nephew and you cannot remember whether he is eight or nine this birthday, how do you proceed? If the present year is 1962 you might subtract nine from it and ask yourself what you were doing in 1953. You remember that that was the year that you moved and had to stay with your parents. Your brother, the boy's father, was also staying there then, and his son had not yet been born. So you conclude your nephew must be eight and not nine. You have reconstructed this fact from your memories of the past. (There are many people, incidentally, in whose minds the past is very poorly organized: it is very easy to confuse the temporal series of events.) So in reconstructing the past you make the best sense of it that you can, in the light of a few events and landmarks that stand out in your memory.

There are two processes at work on memories—on the one hand those that make them fade and disintegrate; on the other hand those that sharpen them, but often by changing them and simplifying them so that they fit in with the rest of your knowledge, and prejudices. The memory traces that you have to search among when answering examination questions will have altered from the traces laid down in your original learning.

Recall usually has to be made in words. Language habits are another source of distortion and modification. People tend to remember in terms of clichés and common phrases. Vocabularies are not unlimited. The report of the original experience is altered to conform to our everyday ways of thinking and talking.

Sources of Error

You can see, therefore, that in the threefold process of learning, storage and retrieval, errors can occur at any of the three stages. (1) There may be errors of observation, such as overlooking, misapprehending, overestimating; (2) errors of memory, such as forgetting, confusion of items, and assimilation to existing ideas; (3) errors in the recall stage, such as filling in gaps, amplification or elaboration of the facts, blending of imagined experiences into the one reported, and using a form of words which is inadequate.

As a horrible example of what can happen to scientific information in the process of communication, Allport and Postman * quote the following:

Dr. G. G. Simpson of the American Museum of Natural History published an account of the geology and paleontology of a region in central Montana. A rigidly correct

* Allport, G. W. and Postman, L. *The Psychology of Rumor.*

summary of the report was issued to the press. The account of the fossil fauna included a description of some small mammals, the oldest known primates, which were about the same size as rats and mice. The report emphasized that these were not in the direct line of descent of modern primates or man, but very ancient representatives of the same broad group of mammals.

About a hundred newspapers published versions of the report, but few had reports that were not seriously wrong scientifically. Typical headlines were:

Monkey Father of Man? Nope a Mouse.
Four-Inch Tree Animal seen as Man's Ancestor.

One account began: "Man instead of having descended from the monkey probably ascended from a four-inch-long tree-dwelling animal which was the ancient grand-daddy of all the mammals on earth today."

A recurrent theme of rats and mice arose because the report said that some of the early mammals were as small as rats and mice. These small vertebrates were made to appear as the direct ancestors of man. The linguistic cliché, "the missing link", was bound to find its way into a story about evolution.

While scientific accuracy is hardly to be expected in popular newspapers, their garbled versions of this scientific report illustrate the distortion and modification that can occur through assimilation to an inadequate framework of ideas. So let the student beware of oversimplifying and distorting ideas to fit in with a stock of set ideas and prejudices. You should be aware of the defects of human beings as recording machines, and try and correct the known sources of error.

As we all know, the testimony of firsthand observers is often at fault. Although persons and concrete objects are reported with 85–90 per cent accuracy, other features, especially quantities and colors, only have 40–50 per cent accuracy. Errors of reporting are most frequent with color, next with position, next with size and least with shape.

Reports are distorted to conform to what witnesses regard as the natural course of events. The kernel of an episode is emphasized and details are omitted. When a verbal report is repeated several times the effect is (1) to establish and reinforce the information, whether true or false and (2) to cause the later reports to be based more on the memory of verbal statements of earlier reports than on the original experience itself. This means that your note-taking must be precise and accurate. Otherwise you will be reinforcing and rehearsing error as you learn and relearn your notes.

In any branch of study, error creeps in as you get further and further away from original records or experimental reports. Sometimes textbooks are at fault in perpetuating errors. Authors of textbooks are not always able to consult original reports, but repeat what is said in other texts. Lecturers who work from the same outline notes year after year may introduce inaccuracies and distort their materials to fit in with a few main ideas. All good scholars, therefore, constantly refresh their knowledge from the source and are aware of all secondhand accounts.

The students who fail examinations are those who lack a sound framework in which to reconstruct their memories. Having forgotten some of the facts, they have to reconstruct their ideas as best they can with limited information—that is they have to fill in the gaps in their knowledge. Given a sound basic knowledge this can often be done, but if some significant part of the framework is wrong or has been forgotten, the reconstruction will be wrong. Mistakes often spring from some basic misunderstanding. If basic facts are well understood this kind of error cannot be made. Once again you can see that the best method of avoiding error in recall is to make sure that you thoroughly understand in the first place.

The Emotional Component in Learning

Learning and remembering are not only matters of the intellect: motives and feelings are involved as well. At school pupils usually like some subjects, and dislike others. Often liking for the teacher and liking for the subject go together. Thus there is an emotional component in learning. If you like the teacher and the subject, you are likely to work hard at it and try to excel at it. In time, as your studies become more specialized, you tend to build up a picture of yourself, a "self-concept", as someone who is, say, good at languages, or poor at mathematics, or hopeless at metalwork, or any kind of manual craft. If you see yourself as a good linguist, you become "involved" in the study of languages, are hurt by any criticism of your linguistic ability, and work particularly hard at your languages. Thus the self-concept becomes a self-fulfilling prophecy: you really do become much better at languages than at other subjects.

Yet, if you are of good average intelligence, you should beware of having too fixed ideas of what you can and what you cannot do. Certainly some people have specific aptitude for particular subjects, such as mathematics, music or art, but often these aptitudes derive in part from training or from the happy accident of having had a good teacher and the experience of success. If therefore you dislike or have difficulty with some part of your work, ask yourself whether the source of your difficulty is not in part your emotional attitude toward the subject or toward the teacher.

It has often been shown that controversial material is more readily learned if it fits in with existing beliefs and attitudes. For example, pro-communist students learned more readily than anti-communist students a list of statements favorable to the U.S.S.R. That material is most easily learned which conforms to existing opinions. The recall of controversial material may also be selective: for instance, theistic students remembered better than atheistic students statements favorable to religion and vice versa. This suggests some resistance to learning and retaining material which is not acceptable to us. Conversely we are very ready to learn from certain sources to which we are favorably inclined, such as a political weekly or a particular author whose work we admire. Even in factual subjects, in which there may not seem to be much room for controversy, there may be some parts of the subject which you regard as old-fashioned or dead wood. Once you begin to develop enthusiasms for certain approaches to your subject, as every active and spirited person does, it becomes rather too easy to dismiss other approaches as worthless and not to bother to learn about them. The hard fact is, however, that if you have to cover a syllabus, you probably cannot afford to neglect any part of it because you think it is unimportant or because you don't like the way it is taught. Some teachers may welcome dissenting opinions on controversial subjects, but others may not, and if you disagree with the "authorized version" the onus lies on you to show exactly why it is wrong and to present an alternative version. Not many students are able enough to do this. Most are probably better advised to develop some tolerance for shortcomings in their teachers and their courses.

Summary

You should thoroughly understand what you are studying. To attain insight you must think and reflect, and relate new information to your existing knowledge.

The "SQ3R" system of study is recommended:

(1) Survey
(2) Asking questions
(3) Reading
(4) Recitation
(5) Review

Meaningful learning is much more efficient than rote learning. Long-term retention is helped by organizing materials and linking them together.

Although general retentiveness cannot be improved, you can improve your methods of memorizing, especially by recitation, attention to meaning, and alertness and concentration. Artificial memory "systems" are seldom useful.

"Overlearning" and avoiding interference are of more assistance in rote than in meaningful learning.

In the threefold process of learning, storage and retrieval, errors can occur at any of the three stages. Make sure that your initial intake of information is precise and accurate, otherwise you may perpetuate errors as you learn and relearn your notes.

There is an emotional component in learning and remembering. Try not to neglect those aspects of your subjects which you dislike, and, if necessary, develop tolerance for your teachers.

For further reading:

Hovland, C. I., "Human Learning and Retention", in Stevens, S. S. (Ed.) *Handbook of Experimental Psychology*. New York. Wiley, 1951.

Gagné, R. M. and Bolles, R. C., *A Review of the Factors in Learning Efficiency in Automatic Teaching*. Galanter, E. (Ed.) New York. Wiley, 1959.

CHAPTER FIVE

READING

Reading is to the mind what exercise is to the body.

STEELE

READING is the most important single skill in study. In English or history perhaps 90 per cent of private study time is taken up in reading. It is known that there are big differences between individuals in their rates of reading and comprehension. Clearly if you can speed up your rate of reading you will save much time. Books and articles, of course, differ in difficulty and in clarity of presentation. And what is difficult for some to read is easy for others. Rate of reading depends on the difficulty of the material and on the purpose of the reading. But there are some students who read even straightforward prose abnormally slowly, and this is certainly a handicap in study. Later in the chapter there is a test of reading speed which will give you some idea of how your reading rate compares with that of others.

Kinds of Reading

First let us consider the different kinds of purposes in reading. We can distinguish:

(1) Reading to master information and content, usually necessarily careful, slow and repeated.
(2) Exploratory reading, as in skimming through a book in order to get a general view of it.
(3) Review reading, as in reading rapidly through a book with which you are already familiar, in order to confirm knowledge.
(4) Reading in order to search for specific information or to answer a specific question.
(5) Critical reading, as in reading a book for review.

76

(6) Reading for enjoyment, as a novel.
(7) Proofreading, when meticulous attention is paid to spelling, punctuation and sentence structure.

A good reader will vary his rate of reading according to his purpose. A novel may be read very quickly, perhaps at 750 words per minute or more, if the reader has no intent to remember, but merely wants to know the fate of the hero or heroine.

A single paragraph or diagram in a textbook, on the other hand, may have to be read through slowly four or five times before it is fully comprehended.

The Nature of Reading

Reading is a very complex process, as is obvious if you think of how long it takes to learn to read. It is useful to think of it as (1) a process of sensory reception, involving skilled eye movements and (2) as a brain process, in which the meaning of the printed symbols is elaborated.

As the eye moves from left to right across the line of print (or from right to left in Arabic, or from top to bottom in Chinese) it progresses in jerks and pauses, then swings from the extreme right to the extreme left to start the next line of reading.

Accurate recording of eye movements demands a camera or an electronic amplifier to record the eye muscle potentials, but you can study them by watching someone else read. Make a small hole in the middle of the page of a newspaper or magazine and watch a friend's eye movements through this hole, as he reads on the other side. Alternatively you can look over the top of a book held vertically by your subject. Since the movement of both eyes is pretty closely coordinated you need only watch one eye. Fix your attention on the outer part of the iris—where the colored zone joins the white. Try and observe the number of pauses per line, and regressions or backward movements in the course of reading a line, the return sweep at the end of a line, and the rhythm and uniformity of progression.

Try and observe also the eye movements of a seven- or eight-year-old child in reading.

In reading a line of print about 4 inches long, most adults make five or six fixations per line, if the reading matter is easy, but more if it is difficult. About two words per fixation are seen. The eye movements between fixations are very quick, and only take up about 10 per cent of the total time, leaving about 90 per cent of the time for intake of information in the pauses. This skill is the result of many years of practice, as the following graph illustrates:

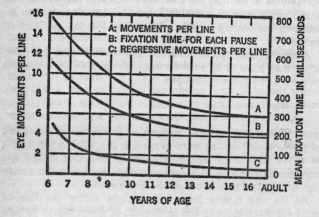

Fig. 11. Increase in reading skill with age

The number of fixations per line of type decreases from fifteen to twenty at age 6 to five or six in educated adults. The length of a fixation decreases from about half a second to about a quarter of a second. The number of regressive movements (as the reader looks back to words previously fixated) decreases from five to less than one.

Here is an illustration of a student's fixations in a line of reading:

```
1        2        3         4      5   8  7  9 6   10
|        |        |         |      |   |  |  | |   |
A common | violation of this rule is illustrated by | the sentence
|        |        |         |      |   |  |  | |   |
.20      .24      .20       .24   .16 .24.24.36.16 .12
```

The lines represent the fixations, the numbers above the lines their order, and the figures below their duration in seconds.

In this record progress is regular until the word "the" is reached, then the eye turns back and wanders over the word "illustrated." Probably the student was not very familiar with the use of "illustrated" in this context.

Improving your Reading

Will training in making more adequate eye movements help to increase your speed of reading? We certainly could take in information at a faster rate. Considering the eye alone, the amount you can take in depends on your visual span, and on the duration of the fixation. How wide is your span? If you maintain your fixation constant on the first word of a line of print, how many words can you see to the right of it without moving the eye? Most people can see about two words distinctly, together with a vague impression of one or two more. That is, they can see about three words at a glance. As there will be only ten to fourteen words in a four-inch line of print it should be possible to cover it, therefore, in three or four fixations, instead of the five or six that are usual. It is also known from experiments that the eye can take in three or four connected words in much less than .25 of a second. If the illumination is good, the actual time required for recognition is only .1–.15 second. Therefore, considering the eye alone, and making allowance for the times between fixations, it should be possible for most people to increase the speed of reading.

We must remember, however, that we read not only with our eyes but with our brains. Fast reading is only possible when we are already very familiar with the language and its content. A familiar word is read as a whole, not by spelling out its letters, and the same is true of common phrases and sentences—they are reacted to as units by adults who are very familiar with them. The printed word thus triggers off speech habits. The rules and grammatical sequences of language enable us to anticipate what is coming. The start of a sentence like "He picked up his knife and fork and started . . ." strongly suggests an ending like "to eat his dinner." In the fast reading of a novel or a newspaper the skilled reader does not bother to read every word, or even every sentence or paragraph. A great deal of the matter may be skipped and yet, recognizing phrases here and there, the experienced reader is able to put together a connected story which is half supplied by the printed page and half by his past experience.

We can see then that speed of reading depends just as much on familiarity and experience, as on the mechanics of eye movements. If long fixations occur it usually means that a word of obscure meaning has been met. Formulas will be fixated for long intervals, as they embody condensed information. Foreign languages are read more slowly. A modern foreign language, such as French, can be read without regressive eye movements. A language like Latin, on the other hand, is not read, but deciphered, with many regressive movements, because of the different order of words in Latin sentences.

There are, therefore, two main sorts of difficulties in reading:

(1) Slow or faulty eye movements.
(2) Difficulties in understanding, arising from a poor vocabulary, or lack of familiarity with the material.

The specific defects found in younger readers include excessive word analysis and word-by-word reading, lip movements and subvocal movements, difficulties with the return sweep, regressions back along the line, and slowness in word recognition. These defects are not very common or severe in older students.

You can find out if you are slow in word recognition by the use of a tachistoscope—an instrument for exposing material for controlled times of very short duration. A good tachistoscope will present material for controlled exposures ranging from about 10 milliseconds (.01 second) up to about 500 milliseconds (.5 second) in 10 millisecond steps.

You can get an approximate idea of your speed of word recognition by getting another person to print in capitals, four or five common six- or seven-letter words in a line on a 3x5 card. The letters should be about a quarter of an inch high. (You must not know what the words are.) The card is then covered with a blank card and you are shown the words for a fraction of a second, by getting someone to slide the cover card upwards and then quickly downwards again. You should be able to recognize at least two words during this brief exposure.

Individual Differences in Reading Rates

There are certainly great differences in reading rates between individuals, whether these result from differences in the eye or in the brain or in both. The speed of twenty students in silent reading of an interesting novel was measured. The mean words read per minute were 336, but the range from the slowest to the fastest reader was 150 to 600 words per minute—that is, the fastest reader read four times as fast as the slowest. The existence of these great differences does suggest that if you are a really slow reader, you may well be able to read faster with practice and training. To get some idea of your performance, a 600-word passage is given below.

Get a watch which has a second hand, and see how long it takes you to read the passage. Read as fast as you can, but do not read so fast that you fail to understand what you are reading. Imagine that you will be asked to explain the gist of the passage after you have read it.

Is It Safe to Invest? * You feel yourself financially able and personally qualified to invest. You can meet the conditions of reasonable stability, reasonable flexibility, and reasonable caution. But nagging doubt remains. Wouldn't you really be better off with your extra cash in a savings account? Or a piece of real estate? In short, is it really safe to invest?

Well, how much safety do you require? Since there are no absolutely sure things anywhere, safety must be looked at as a matter of degree. There are no guarantees of success in stock ownership, no guarantees against loss. Even the thoughtful, conscientious investor can be taken to the cleaners.

It should be remembered, however, that investment in stocks is a way of sharing in the profit potential of American industry. Is the American economy safe? It seems to be. Since 1900 it has been rising in productivity at an average rate of 4 per cent per year. Our Gross National Product is now nearly $480 billion. By 1965, according to quite conservative estimates, it is expected to rise 30 per cent to some $535 billion. A few hard-headed star-gazers among our economists feel it may go as high as $600 billion and perhaps to $700 billion by 1970. (In the early Thirties it was only $56 billion—less than the 1959 Federal budget.) Should these peaks in fact be reached, or even approached, the likely result would be an unexampled level of national prosperity.

* From *How to Invest Safely and for Profit* by Adolph Suehsdorf, Crest Book d376, © 1960, Fawcett Publications Inc., Greenwich, Connecticut.

For corporations, prosperity is reflected in earnings. For stockholders, it is reflected in a larger share of these earnings through increased dividends, or in capital gains—a rise in the value of the stock in the open market owing to the pressure of investors who anticipate further earnings by the corporation and wish to get aboard.

This generally upward trend is, in fact, the course the market has taken in this century. [In only 29 years—from 1930 to the end of 1959—the value of stocks listed on the New York Stock Exchange has zoomed from $49 billion to more than $307 billion.]

Of course, none of this means that the economy is impervious to setbacks or depressions. We have had them before and, chances are, we will have them again. An economy is a subtle and, to a considerable extent, still unknown combination of forces which produces prosperity only when a certain balance is maintained among them. Until all the factors establishing the balance are understood and controlled, dislocations can and will occur.

It also follows that depression is pervasive. Stock values are a sensitive—and sometimes nervous—barometer of economic weather, but they are not the only gauge affected in times of stress. The bottom has been known to fall out of the real-estate market. And insurance companies and savings institutions, both of which invest heavily in real estate, mortgages, and securities to obtain the earnings they pay out in interest, cannot escape the consequences of a national depression either.

In their pleasure at seeing banks raise their interest rate on savings to 3¼ per cent, as many have done in the past few years, people are inclined to forget that there was a time when banks paid 4 per cent. But somewhere along the line, in response to economic factors and the available return on investment, there was a decline to a 2 per cent rate from which we are only now emerging. What price safety?

If you believe in the essential safety of the American economy, if you have faith in the ability of American business to flourish in the future as it has in the past, investment as a technique for making your extra money make money is safe.

You can get an idea of your reading speed by comparing

your time with the times of a sample of university students given below:

Percentile	Time
90 (Fastest 10 percent)	1 minute or less
75 (Fastest 25 percent)	2 mins. 30 secs. or less
50 (Middle)	3 mins. 30 secs.
25 (Slowest 25 percent)	3 mins. 50 secs. or more
10 (Slowest 10 percent)	5 mins. or more

You will see that the most common time is about 3½ minutes—a rate of less than 200 words a minute. This passage contains some very factual paragraphs, and many figures. It is thus of moderate difficulty, and needs to be read with close attention. It may be of interest to the reader that it took me (the author) 2½ minutes to read and understand the passage, and that I am as a rule an exceptionally fast reader. I suspect that those students who returned times of less than a minute had not properly assimilated the meaning of the passage.

If you had no real difficulty in understanding the content of the passage, but needed more than 4 minutes in which to read it, you might well try to increase your reading speed.

Methods of Improving Reading

If you think that you are a slow reader, what can you do to improve your speed? First you should ask yourself why you do read slowly—the causes may be: talking to yourself as you read, an inadequate vocabulary, an inability to vary your rate of reading to suit the material and your purpose, or just a habit of reading slowly. Some people, of course, are temperamentally more cautious than others, and like to proceed slowly and thoughtfully in all things, including reading. Some slow readers may be good readers, and some fast readers poor readers—it is how much you can understand and remember that counts. It is no good trying to read faster than you can assimilate ideas. Nevertheless if your reading speed for *easy* material is less than about 200 words per minute, you would be well advised to learn to read more quickly. It is of little use to attempt to control your eye movements directly—the attention that you will have to pay to your eyes will distract you from the task of reading proper. The most useful procedure is just to practice reading faster.

If you move your lips in reading you are bound to be a slow reader. No one can speak at more than about 125 words a minute, whereas you should be able to read two or three times as fast. The best cure for lip movements and other small accompanying movements of the vocal organs is to read so fast that such movements are impossible.

In order to develop speed, a daily period of systematic practice is necessary, extending over at least three or four weeks. Arrange to spend 15 or 20 minutes each day on this task. As you must be absolutely constant in your practice, it is best to choose a time at which you will seldom be interrupted, such as the time immediately before going to bed each night.

The best materials to start on are fairly short easy selections such as you may find in your daily newspaper or in some magazines. Short articles are very suitable.

Read each article through as quickly as you can without sacrificing comprehension. Time yourself accurately for each article. Estimate the number of words in the article by multiplying the number of lines by the average number of words per line. Work out your rate of reading in words per minute.

Keep a chart or a graph of your reading rate. After two weeks of such practice you should have both increased your rate, and stabilized it on the new higher level.

Look at the sample record. You will see that there is fluctuation from day to day—as is only to be expected since the material read will differ in difficulty. Over the whole period, however, there is a definite improvement, the final rate being about 100 words per minute faster than the starting rate.

By means of this constant and extended practice slow readers should be able to increase their speed of reading by at least 50 per cent for easy material.

Next you should start practicing on harder material, such as your textbooks. You must now be doubly careful not to read so fast that you fail to get the meaning. Remember that technical books may have to be read relatively slowly, whereas texts in English or history may usually be read at a faster rate. Thus you will need to keep separate records for literary and for technical materials. Continue your practice until you flatten out on a new higher level of performance,

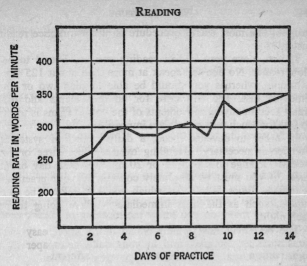

Fig. 12. Improvement in speed of reading with daily periods of timed practice

and then carry on until the higher rate is fully established and consolidated.

Methods for Increasing Reading Speed

Several mechanical methods of controlling the rate of reading have been developed. In one such method, the material to be read is placed on a revolving drum and exposed one line at a time through an aperture. Another method involves the use of special films. A page of reading is projected on to a screen, and one phrase after another stands out brightly from the rest of the page. The rate of projection can be slowed down or speeded up to meet the needs of the trainees. Mechanical devices are, however, in no way superior to the method of timed practice described above, at least for mature students. The success of any method in fact results largely from the interest and motivation engendered. Any mechanical method of speeding up rate of reading can be only partially successful if the slow reading results from a poor vocabulary or poor understanding. Eye movements in fact are symptoms, rather than causes of difficulty in reading. It may be more sensible, therefore, to increase your reading rate indirectly by improving your vocabulary and methods of reading.

Improving your Vocabulary

There are immense individual differences in size of vocabulary. In common speech only about 3,000 words are used with any great frequency. Academic texts, however, and particularly scientific texts, use terms which are not ordinarily employed in common speech. Apart from the technical vocabulary common to each separate discipline, there are many words and phrases which occur very frequently in textbooks. Many are of Greek or Latin origin. Here is a sample of 150 recurring words, nearly all of Greek or Latin origin. How many do you know the meaning of? Mark each word either Yes, No, or Doubtful.

abstraction	achromatic	afferent
affective	agent	aggregate
ambiguous	anthropomorphic	antecedent
antithesis	atrophy	avocation
bevel	binary	binaural
binocular	bureaucracy	
calibrate	casuistry	category
causal	cognition	complementary
concept	concomitant	contiguity
corollary		
decrement	differentiate	discontinuous
discrepant	discrete	doctrinaire
ductile	dynamic	
empirical	endogenous	environment
equilibrium	equivalent	equivocal
ergonomics	extrapolate	extrinsic
facilitate	fiducial	florescent
fractionate	functional	
genetic	gradation	gradient
heterogeneity	heuristic	hierarchy

homogeneous   hortatory   hypothesis

ideology   impairment   implicit
inhibit   insidious   integration
interpolate   intrinsic   invariant
inverse

kinesthesis   kinetic

labile   labyrinth   lacuna
laminated   latency   linear

malleable   mastication   medial
metamorphosis   minuscule   modulate
monotonic   motive

nativism   neologism   nosology
null

    occlude   ogive
oblique   ontogenetic   optimal
olfaction
ostensible

palliative   palpable   paradigm
paradox   parameter   peripheral
phylogeny   postulate   pragmatism
presumptive   probability   prognostic
putative

qualitative   quantitative

radical   rarefaction   ratiocination
recidivist   reciprocal   replicate
retroaction

sanction   satiation   semantic
sequential   sinusoidal   somatic
soporific   status   structural
sudorific   synchronize   syndrome

tactual   tangential   tangible
teleology   temporal   tentative
therapy   topology   toxicity
trophism

| ubiquitous | undulation | unilateral |
| utilitarian | | |

| vascular | variable | veridical |
| visceral | volition | |

xenophobia

You should know the meaning of at least 100 of the 150 words if you are to read textbooks, particularly scientific textbooks, without difficulty.

The best way of improving your vocabulary is to read widely in your field of study. In a new field of study, read some of the excellent introductory texts which are now increasingly becoming available as paperbacks. Make summaries or abstracts of parts that interest you, and try and use new words in your own writing and speech.

Word Derivation

Since so many academic words come from Latin and Greek, it may help you to systematize your knowledge of their roots. The following sample list, comprising eight Latin and three Greek words, provides the roots for over 2,000 English words:

		Derivatives
venio	(I come)	contravention, intervention, subvent, advent.
dico	(I say)	diction, interdict, dictaphone, dictionary.
duco	(I lead)	ductile, induct, inductive.
facio	(I make)	fact, satisfaction, manufacture, facsimile.
mitto	(I send)	intermittent, missile, emit, emissary.
plico	(I fold)	replica, duplicate, implicate, complicate.
tendo	(I stretch)	tension, tendon, subtend, tensile.
specio	(I look)	spectator, spectrum, inspect, aspect.
grapho	(I write)	graph, graphic, graphology, telegraph.
logos	(word)	logic, biology, geology, logarithm.
skopeo	(I look)	microscope, telescope, scope.

Even without a knowledge of Latin you will be able to make a pretty good guess at word meanings if you know (*a*) some of the more common roots like those given above and (*b*) commonly used prefixes and suffixes.

Some Common Prefixes

a or ab	(Latin ab)	—from, as avert, absolve.
a or ad	(Latin ad)	—to, as ascend, adhere.
a	(Greek a)	—not, as achromatic.
bi	(Latin bi)	—two, as bichloride, binocular.
co or com	(Latin com)	—together, with, as coauthor, committee.
de	(Latin de)	—from, down, as depart, descend.
dis	(Latin dis)	—apart, as disintegrate, dissect.
en	(Latin in)	—as enfold, engrave.
epi	(Greek epi)	—upon, as epidermis, epicyclic.
hyper	(Greek hyper)	—over, as hyperbola, hypercritical.
hypo	(Greek hypo)	—under, as hypodermic, hypochondria.
in	(Latin in)	—not, as inability, inoperative.
also il, im, ir		as illiberal, immodest, irreverent.
pre	(Latin pre)	—before, as predetermine, prejudge.
pro	(Latin or Greek pro)	—forward, for, in favor of, as project, proconsul, pro-German.
re	(Latin re)	—back, again, as regress, reread.
sub	(Latin sub)	—under, as submarine, subdivide.
trans	(Latin trans)	—across, through, as transit, transparent.

Some Common Suffixes

-able	—tending to, able to, as friable, readable.
-al	—pertaining to, as musical, personal.
-ant or ent	—in the process of doing, as militant, respondent.
-ise or ize	—to make, cause to resemble, as socialize, anglicize.
-ive	—having the character of, as festive, cognitive.
-ment	—denoting result or action, as achievement, fulfillment.
-ous	—presence of a quality in abundance, as verminous, studious.
-ule	—diminutive, as granule, module.

From a knowledge of roots, prefixes and suffixes, you will often be able to dissect new and unfamiliar words. Real understanding of word usage, however, only comes after seeing words used in a variety of contexts. Hence extensive reading is always desirable.

Other things you can to do improve your vocabulary are:

(1) Use a good dictionary. Look up any words of which you are unsure at once.

(2) Use new words in your own speech and writing.

(3) Get a glossary of the technical terms used in your fields of study. Several such glossaries are available as paperbacks, in such fields as anatomy, psychology, etc.

(4) If you want to be really systematic, use a card system. Write down important new words, singly, on small (3 × 5 inches) cards. Include definitions, synonyms and derivations. File the cards alphabetically and look through them at intervals.

Methods of Reading

You should remind yourself here of the SQ3R method. Remember the advice to get a general view of a chapter of a textbook before studying it in detail. Particular topics can then be seen in their proper perspective, and it is easier to judge the relative importance of each.

As you read, make sure that you can pick out the main ideas expressed in each paragraph. In textbooks, many authors begin a paragraph by first setting out the main idea, and then explaining it, producing supporting evidence, and ending with a summary sentence. Often a summary of each chapter is included at the end. If you are in any doubt about the main points the author is trying to make, concentrate on the summary first, filling in the details later. Or try jotting down the main facts or ideas included in each paragraph.

If you have a real interest in your subjects you will soon develop opinions of your own. A definite "line" is often a great stimulus to study. Reading becomes much more critical and you ask: "Does this agree with what I already know?" "Is this a suitable procedure?" "What evidence has the author for this statement?" "Has the author selected among his facts in order to build up a case?" "Can the facts be interpreted in another way?"

At the same time beware of rashly pursuing certain favorite views to the neglect of all else. In many long-standing controversies, such as the relative importance of heredity and environment, advances in knowledge are made by reconciling opposing statements, rather than by hotly pushing one extreme position and militantly opposing the opposite one.

Buy the Books you Need

It should hardly be necessary to say that it is useless to improve your methods of reading unless you own the textbooks which are necessary for your work. Yet in my experience there are many students who will not buy even the basic textbooks for their courses, and many more who are poor buyers of books.

It is absolute folly not to buy at least basic textbooks. Books are to the student what tools are to the tradesman—it is impossible to do any useful work without them. To maintain a student at a college or university costs some thousands of dollars a year, yet sometimes this expenditure is nullified because the student will not spend fifty dollars per annum on the requisite books.

Few things distinguish more sharply between good and poor students than the ownership of books. A serious student is always prepared to make the necessary financial sacrifice to obtain the books he requires; the weak student thinks he cannot afford them. True, many texts, particularly scientific texts, are expensive, and for this reason you should look through them before buying them to make sure that they are suitable in content and in level of difficulty. This applies even to "officially" recommended texts. Teachers sometimes recommend texts which are too difficult. Sometimes the official list of books has not been revised and brought up to date. Usually alternative texts are available. Therefore discuss the matter carefully with your teachers, and make sure you buy the best books for your purpose.

In many subjects a great many new books come out each year, very few of which are either well written or of any permanent value. Your teachers will be your best guides to this mass of new literature, but usually you will be well advised to confine your first purchases to standard texts, and to build up a small library of well-tried works.

Use of the Library

Knowing where to find information when you need it is

almost as important as learning itself. Therefore you should spend a day or more thoroughly familiarizing yourself with your library and its resources.

Make sure of the location of the card catalogue, reference books, bound and unbound journals, and of the shelves and stacks that contain the books in your own subject.

Most libraries use the Dewey Decimal system of classification. There are nine main classes, and a tenth class designated O for general works and encyclopedias:

000–099	General works
100–199	Philosophy and Psychology
200–299	Religion
300–399	Sociology
400–499	Philology
500–599	Science
600–699	Useful Arts
700–799	Fine Arts
800–899	Literature
900–999	History

The first digit gives the general classification or major division. The second digit permits ten further subdivisions, etc., so that together with the use of decimals, minute discriminations between fields is possible, and all books on specific topics can be shelved next to each other.

The Library of Congress system is also widely used; it has twenty-six main divisions, denoted by an initial letter. A further letter permits subdivision, and the letters are then followed by numerals.

A	Encyclopedias and reference books.
B	Philosophy, Psychology, Religion.
C	Antiquities, Biography.
D	History
E-F	American History.
G	Geography, Anthropology.
H	Social Sciences, Economics, Sociology.
I	Political Science.
L	Education.
M	Music.
N	Fine Arts.
P	Language and Literature.
Q	Science.

R	Medicine.
S	Agriculture and Veterinary Science.
T	Technology.
U	Military Science.
V	Naval Science.
Z	Books and Libraries, Bibliographies.

The main divisions are subdivided thus:
Q Science, QA Mathematics, QB Astronomy, QC Physics, QD Chemistry, QE Geology, QH Natural History, QK Botany, QL Zoology, QM Anatomy, QP Physiology, QR Bacteriology.

All libraries are extensively indexed by author, by title and by subject. The author index is the most commonly used. In a library of any size you will find it essential to have the initials of the author as well as the surname. Get into the habit of noting down the titles of books in standard form as:

Miller, G. A., *Language and Communication*, New York, McGraw-Hill, 1951.

or

Machin, K. E., "Transducers", in Donaldson, P. E. K. (Ed.) *Electronic Apparatus for Biological Research*, London, Butterworth, 1958.

Journal references should also be taken down in standard form:

Bruner, J. S., "The Act of Discovery", *Harvard Educational Review*, 31, 1961, 21–32.

If you always note down author, title, journal, volume number, year and page numbers in this fashion, you will save much time in consulting and quoting references.

In nearly all fields of study some hundreds of new books and thousands of articles appear each year. How is it possible to keep abreast of this vast literature? In many subjects, regular abstracts of the literature are published, as Chemical Abstracts, Biological Abstracts, etc., which give short summaries of published articles, classified under different headings. Even more valuable, particularly to research students, are the annual reviews now published in some subjects, in which experts in various fields summarize, review and criticize recent publications.

Broaden your Knowledge

Nowadays there is too much specialization and departmentalism of knowledge. Few people can master fully more than one specialized field, but the best students do not confine their reading too narrowly to their special subjects. An educated person used to be expected to know something of history, current affairs and politics, literature and fine arts, philosophy and religion. It is now becoming increasingly necessary that he should also know something of science and scientific method, and of mathematics and statistics.

Summary

Reading is the most important skill in study. Good readers learn to vary their rate of reading to suit their purposes.

Reading involves making complicated patterns of eye movements, as well as understanding what you read. You should observe the eye movements made in reading—the jumps, fixations, regressions and sweeps.

Difficulties in reading may be the result of faulty eye movements, or of a poor vocabulary or lack of understanding. If you think your reading of easy prose materials is slow you can speed your rate by regular periods of timed practice, charting your progress on a graph. This method is just as good as mechanical methods of speeding up reading.

Improvement can also be effected by improving your vocabulary. This is best done by doing more reading and writing, but it may also help to systematize your knowledge of Greek and Latin words, from which many learned words are derived. And use a good dictionary.

Learn to read intelligently and critically. Make sure of the general plan of what you are reading, and distinguish the main ideas from the details.

Make sure you are thoroughly familiar with your library —particularly the card index and reference system. Don't rely on the library for basic texts. It is absolute folly not to own the necessary books for your courses.

CHAPTER SIX

NOTES AND LECTURES

The palest ink is better than the most retentive
memory.

CHINESE PROVERB

TAKING notes at lectures and other classes will be dealt with
first, and then the making of notes and outlines from books.

Some students may need to be convinced that they should
take lecture notes at all. The reasons for taking notes are:

(1) A permanent record is constructed which is invaluable
for reviewing and subsequent relearning.

(2) The permanent record helps to overcome our limitations
in recording and storing information. Although a careful and intelligent listener may be able to recall the
general structure and arguments of a lecture immediately
afterwards, much of the detail fades very rapidly. This
is particularly true of factual expository lectures, which
include tables, figures and formulas. Our memory span,
even for familiar material, cannot cope with a mass of
factual detail even for a short period, and since education is concerned with long-term retention, a written
record is essential.

(3) Note-taking itself, as it involves vision and muscular and
kinesthetic senses, as well as hearing, may facilitate
learning. Although it may appear that note-taking necessarily distracts the attention of the listener from the
speaker's words—note-takers are always "lagging" behind the speaker, that is, writing down what he has just
said, while listening to what he is now saying—writing
and listening are not really incompatible. It is possible
to do two things at once, provided that one of the
things has been reduced to the level of an automatic
skill. So it is possible to keep your thoughts with the

lecturer while writing down enough of what he has said
to be able to reconstruct it later.

(4) To clinch the argument, research studies show that note-
takers do a lot better in tests and examinations than
those who don't take notes. In one experiment, for
example, in a test some weeks after the original lecture
note-takers scored about 65 per cent, non-note-takers
only 25 per cent. The note-takers had been able to go
over and rehearse their notes in the interim, while the
others had only their remote memories to rely on.

Notebooks

The technique of note-taking is dealt with at length later.
First we must consider different kinds of notebooks and filing systems. Not many students give enough time and thought
to these rather mundane matters, which are, nevertheless, of
the first importance. Consider that, in whatever branch of
study you are engaged, you must learn to deal in an orderly
fashion with a mass of books and papers. Some time each
day necessarily has to be spent in sorting and classifying
notes and papers, even if you find this activity trivial and
distasteful. I fancy that there are some who scorn to stoop
to the mechanical contrivances which suggest shop and office
and business routine. These mechanical devices have, however, been devised to minimize effort in this humdrum sphere.
Besides, there are times in the day when we are all at a low
ebb of neural potency, when a little routine activity may
be desirable.

A notebook on any subject should not be something in
which you take lecture notes only, but a depository of information on the subject from all sources. You should fill
out your lecture notes from your textbook reading, and add
thoughts and critical comments of your own, together with
illustrations, other evidence, etc. This means that the notebook has to be a certain size and that you must leave plenty
of room for the comments, diagrams or illustrations which
may be added later. Never try to economize on paper.

The problem which has to be solved is something like
this. You have to take notes in perhaps ten or twelve separate
courses and to have these notes readily available both at
your workplace and at your residence, which means transporting them frequently between workplace and residence.
One possible solution is to buy a set of bound exercise

books, one for each course or topic. Exercise books, however, usually turn out to be insufficiently flexible. Additions to the notes on a given topic may be some pages away from the original, so that a logical sequence is hard to preserve and the student has to leaf backwards and forwards to re-read a single topic. This difficulty may be overcome by writing lecture notes on one side of the paper only, and leaving plenty of space for subsequent additions, but even so the system is, by general consent, too rigid and clumsy—and may entail transporting six or eight separate exercise books each day; and if you should forget the appropriate book there is no easy way of adding to it the new notes you have taken.

Some kind of loose-leaf system is better. The most common system includes a loose-leaf notebook with rings. The notebook is set up with tabular dividers, one for each of the subjects you are taking. A pad of fresh paper, with holes ready punched, is kept at the rear of the notebook. You take your notes on the pad, beginning a fresh sheet for each topic, and then file under the appropriate tab within the body of the notebook. At intervals, or at the conclusion of a course, you can take out the notes on each topic and file them away in a folder or binder of some kind.

This is quite a sensible system. The same loose-leaf notebook can be used for all your classes, and you only have to transport one notebook between your workplace and residence. The disadvantage of the system is that if you lose the notebook (as sometimes happens) you lose the accumulated work of weeks or months. A safer practice is to take out notes from the notebook every few days and file these away, each topic in its separate binder or folder. Another disadvantage of the ring system is that it does not stand normal wear and tear. The paper around the holes becomes torn, sheets come adrift from the notebook, leading to untidiness and confusion. The remedy is to stick small reinforcing circles round the holes in the paper—a tedious and unnecessary task.

A loose-leaf system which does not rely on rings and punched holes is neater and less time-consuming. Perhaps the best procedure is to have a folder with an easily manipulated clip which holds a good supply of fresh paper. Notes are made in this folder in the classroom. Every few days the notes are taken out and filed away in folders or spring-back binders. The only disadvantage of the system is that you may have to transport your files from residence to workplace if you want to consult recent notes.

At all events any system is better than no system. Some students take notes on any old piece of paper or on the backs of envelopes. These are then creased or folded into their pockets and may be lost or forgotten. Eventually, as examinations approach, some effort may be made to reduce the available scraps to order, usually with very little success. Such lack of system is really carrying the amateur tradition too far.

Whatever system you decide on, it is worth going to a good commercial stationer and examining the notebooks, filing systems and other aids, and thinking about how the available equipment can be adapted to your needs. Think also of how you are going to transport books and papers from residence to workplace. The conventional briefcase is usually far too small for the purpose—particularly if you have to transport one or two large textbooks. A small suitcase, or rucksack or large leather bag may be desirable. Don't be deterred from taking around with you the books and papers that you need by the mere physical difficulties of carrying them.

Lectures

Most lectures are frankly expository, that is, their purpose is to convey information, subject-matter or techniques. You may think that this can often be done better by a textbook. In reading a book you can go back over difficult passages and proceed at your own pace; in a lecture you cannot go back, and must habituate yourself to the rate at which the lecturer presents his material.

Lectures are sometimes criticized as a passive form of learning: the lecturer speaks, the class listens, and makes notes. Normally the lecturer is not interrupted or asked questions, but proceeds at a uniform pace, and does not know whether he is being fully understood or not. Sometimes questions and discussion may be invited, but normally verbal communication is one-way. Most lecturers, however, unless they are socially very obtuse, are aware of their audience's reactions, and realize when they need to repeat themselves, recapitulate, or supply fresh illustrations or examples.

Listening to a lecture need not be a passive affair, in which the lecturer's utterance is patiently recorded, a process much more efficiently done by a tape recorder. The lecturer's words should be generating thought processes in you. You should be thinking about what he is saying, making personal examples and applications, reacting in a critical fashion or trying to link up the discourse with your existing body of knowledge.

The impact of a lecture is usually greater than that of a book, because enthusiasms and attitudes are more readily communicated in the personal situation. Lecturers usually believe that no one textbook (unless it is their own) covers the subject adequately, and that they can give a better and more detailed account of particular topics than any book. Important experiments may be hidden away in inaccessible journals, for example, and it may be necessary to quote the procedure and findings in some detail, in order to illustrate some general principle or law. Moreover, a good lecturer can organize and integrate the various aspects of a subject more effectively than a book, and give a treatment more adapted to the needs of a particular audience. In some subjects new knowledge comes in rapidly, and there is inevitably a time-lag of a few years before this new knowledge becomes sufficiently established to be incorporated in textbooks. In new fields a lecture can be nearer to recent research than a textbook.

In educational methods research, lectures usually turn out to be just as effective as other teaching methods, judged by examination results, and since a lecturer can address 200 students almost as easily as two, it is likely to continue as one of the principal methods of instruction. There is, moreover, an advantage in a whole class being subjected to the same instruction at the same time: their common experience gives a basis for subsequent discussion. And even when you go to a lecture and understand very little of it, at least you are becoming aware of deficiencies in your knowledge. I have attended lectures which I believe very few of the audience fully understood, but at least they became aware of areas of ignorance and were able to take down enough notes to help them to make a start in tackling the subject.

Where to Sit

In many lecture halls the acoustics are bad, so that if you sit at the back it may be a strain to hear the lecturer, and your attention may become intermittent. Moreover, you may be distracted by having the rest of the audience in your field of view. The best place to sit is in the middle towards the front, where you can see and hear easily. Believe it or not, those who sit in this position usually do better than those who sit at the back. This is partly the result of the physical advantage of being reasonably near to the lecturer, and to the blackboard, and partly the result of subtle psychological factors. Those sitting towards the front are usually keen students who quite enjoy going to the lecture; those at the back are more likely to dislike the lecture or the lecturer, and therefore partially dissociate themselves from the proceedings by sitting as far back as possible.

The Amount of Notes to Take

There is no simple answer to the question of how full your notes should be. Lecture notes range all the way from the verbatim account to the barest of outlines. Note-taking usually lies somewhere between these extremes. The amount you need to take down will depend on:

(1) The content of the lecture—a very factual expository lecture may necessitate a great quantity of notes.
(2) Whether or not you are familiar with the topic—the less familiar you are with the subject the fuller your notes will need to be.
(3) Whether the information is readily available in a textbook or elsewhere—if no other source is readily available, notes may have to be full.

In taking notes there are, then, three courses open to you: (1) you can take down as much of the lecture as possible, (2) you can take outline notes, including, in more detail, definitions, tables of figures, graphs etc., as may seem necessary, (3) you can take a skeleton outline only—or no notes at all. The middle course (2) is generally recommended, but let us examine the pros and cons of each course:

(1) To take down every word is impossible unless you are a shorthand writer, since most speakers utter about 130 words a minute. But it is possible to take very full notes, since most lecturers have occasional pauses, or clean the blackboard or use visual aids. All but the most factual lectures, however, include redundant material in

the form of introductory remarks, repetition and re-emphasis, multiple illustrations, and occasional stories and anecdotes, and other "connective tissue". There is no point in taking down these things at any great length, even if you hold the (mistaken) belief that lecturers, being also examiners, like to get their own words and phrases back.

Those who take notes at very great length usually do so as a kind of safety measure, when they cannot fully understand the lecture and so cannot discriminate the important from the unimportant. Everyone may occasionally find himself in this difficulty, and it is then reasonable to take full notes, and to try and clarify the matter after the lecture. The chief argument against *habitually* taking very full notes is that the hectic scribbler has no time to think and follow the general argument, and so may lose the meaning of the lecture as a whole. Moreover, when he comes to review and relearn the notes, many pages of continuous writing are hard to organize and to commit to memory. Points stand out, and are much more easily visualized in memory, when notes are indented, numbered or labelled, well spaced out and interspersed with diagrams. This is very well understood by the writers of introductory textbooks, who break up their text with subheadings, diagrams, "boxes", and tables. The same kind of variety of visual pattern is desirable in your notes: pages of unrelieved handwriting present a visual field which is too homogeneous to be readily organized and memorized.

(2) Outline notes have this very advantage which full notes lack: they are much more readily visualized and reconstructed in memory. Since the student is not writing all the time, he can listen more intelligently, and think about what the lecturer is saying. You must, in fact, be able to understand a lecture in order to make good outline notes. If you merely put down each striking phrase or interesting point as it occurs the resulting notes may be very disjointed.

At the very least you should ensure that the transition from one topic to the next is well emphasized in the spacing of your notes. Use headings and subheadings, and leave plenty of room for elaboration or expansion after the lecture. In taking notes, often a single word will be enough to remind you of an illustration or example, so that you can reconstruct what was said at the end of the lecture or on the same day. A week later, however, you may have forgotten the context or lost the point of the illustration. Hence you must go over outline notes on the same day. This does not mean recopying, which would be a terrible waste of time, but running rapidly through the notes, making sure that their meaning is clear, adding an additional word or phrase here and there, and clearing up any points you may have been unsure about. Sometimes it may be possible to do this in the last ten minutes of a lecture, when some lecturers obligingly summarize the main points they have been trying to make and invite questions. More often you will have to do it later in the same day.

(3) The third course is to take no notes at all, or only the barest outline. This is obvious folly in an expository lecture which is crammed with facts—unless the same facts are available in a textbook. It may be a sensible procedure in a literary or philosophical or inspirational lecture which is designed to stimulate rather than to instruct. If you already have an extensive background of knowledge in a subject, it may appear more important to follow the argument closely, and to think about it, than to take notes. But impressions fade very quickly, so that some kind of skeleton outline is required even here. And since writing is, after all, an automatic process, brief notes need not distract attention from the content and thought of the lecture. In quite a short talk, memories and impressions crowd in so fast that only a few of the most vivid and recent impressions are subsequently recalled. Consider the common sort of "tutorial" discussion, in which someone reads a short paper for twenty minutes, followed by forty minutes of group discussion. Unless the speaker or the chairman has made a careful list of the main topics dealt with, the group nearly always discusses at length only a small part of the paper, and entirely neglects some important questions and issues. So it is in lectures. Unless you take some notes, certain details will become sharpened and emphasized, others will fade completely and inaccuracies and oversimplifications will occur. The experimental psychology of memory has demonstrated in quite devastating fashion the limitations of human beings as

recording instruments. You cannot afford not to make notes.

Organization

For an hour's lecture most lecturers work from about three pages of notes. They will have a structure of headings and subheadings, and the class, in their turn, have to discover and reproduce this structure in their own notes. Some lecturers obligingly read out or list on the blackboard the main topics with which they intend to deal, in the belief that they should "say what they are going to say, say it, and then say what they have said". More often it is left to the audience to discover the structure of the lecture.

To do this intelligently needs familiarity with the style of particular lecturers. Most lecturers give fairly obvious indications when they pass from one major heading to the next, either by pausing, or by saying "Turning now to . . ." or some such introductory phrase, so that, even if you have had no preview of the lecture, there should be little difficulty in picking out the main headings.

It is rather more difficult to decide what you must write down, and what you can omit. Lecturers stress important points by pauses, by slowing down their rate to dictation speed, by inflection of the voice, by repetition, by increased loudness and other forms of emphasis. By watching for these signs you should be better able to select the important points and to omit the mere connective tissue, although a really intelligent abstract of a lecture naturally implies that the listener is following the argument and can see for himself why some points are more important than others.

In fact it is wrong to think that your job in attending a lecture is confined to constructing a set of notes which will very closely resemble the lecturer's own notes. There are indeed some lecturers who proceed at almost dictation speed, dictate main headings, number all subheadings serially, and frequently pause to dictate definitions and summary sentences. This method ensures that everyone in the class will have the same cut-and-dried account in his notebook, and may be appropriate to the introductory stages of some subjects. But it is perhaps fortunate that the majority of lecturers are not so didactic in their methods. They are usually more concerned to state questions and problems precisely, to review the evidence, examine its credibility, to reconcile conflicting evidence, to draw conclusions and discuss implications. It is as well to remember that this is the natural sequence of ideas in critical argument, and ensure that your notes follow a similar logical sequence, wherever possible.

Use of Symbols and Abbreviations

Since your notes will usually only be read by you, you can reasonably employ any symbols or shorthand devices which will help you to take notes more quickly. Common symbols and abbreviations which are generally useful include:

e.g. —for example
cf. —compare, remember in this context
n.b. —note well—this is important
$\therefore$ —Therefore
$\because$ —Because
$\supset$ —implies—it follows from this that . . .
$>$ —greater than
$<$ —less than
$=$ —equals—is the same as
$\neq$ —does not equal—is not the same as

Improving your Ability to Take Notes

Note-taking is a skill which will improve with practice, but you will make much more rapid progress if you have some information about the nature of your errors and omissions. To get this information you will need the cooperation of two or three others who are attending the same course. Form a work group with two or three others, and examine and compare the notes taken on the same lecture by each individual. Note especially any inaccuracies and omissions.

In addition see if you can agree on the characteristics which good notes should possess. These are some of the points you might look for:

> *General Form of Notes*
> Notebook of unsuitable size
> Pages overfilled
> Notes too spread out
> Notes too compact
> Handwriting illegible

Organization
Not in outline form
Hard to see organization
Insufficient use of headings,
numbers, indentation

Phrasing and Content
Too much detail
Too meager
Wordiness
Meaning unclear
Important ideas missed out
Graphs or tables omitted or incorrect

When you have agreed on a check list along these lines, each set of notes should be assessed by each individual, checking each of the points which are at fault. When this has been done, you should have a clearer idea of what you have been doing wrong, and how you should set about improving your notes.

Taking Notes from Books

Outlining, writing summaries and underlining the text are all practices which can help to reinforce your knowledge of a topic, the schematic outline which you yourself have constructed being more readily visualized and assimilated than the text itself. In order to make outline notes you must analyze and closely attend to the book: the activity itself involves you in an active process of learning. For purposes of review, it is much easier to master your three or four pages of notes than the twenty or thirty pages of the chapter itself.

Written summaries should be supplemented by underlining and writing comments on the text itself. This is a practice which schools and libraries naturally frown upon, but which is helpful and efficient in the books which you own yourself. You may of course be prevented from reselling the book, since a book with underlining is useless to anyone except the person who does the underlining. But don't let this deter you. The most common fault is to underline too much. It is seldom necessary to underline the text horizontally—usually it will suffice to put a vertical line in the margin to mark important passages. Intelligent underlining can only be done after you have read the material through as a whole. Following the SQ3R system, you should first read quickly through to get the general picture, then, on the second reading, underline the main ideas and important details.

Underlining by itself may be a more efficient procedure than writing summaries, unless the summaries are adequate and accurate. Practice and training are needed for you to become skilled in outlining. Many students in fact do not make book outlines, and, assuming that you own a copy of a book, and that the author provides summaries of each chapter, there may seem little point in making an outline of your own. The case is different, of course, if you do not own an important book nor have ready access to it. Then there is a clear case for making fairly copious notes for later reference. But it is obviously more efficient to buy all the books that you need in order to save yourself the labor of transcription.

Research shows, however, that the best way to master textbooks is to train yourself to make brief outline notes, selecting the important points and avoiding inaccuracies. Many textbooks are set out with headings and subheadings, each paragraph beginning with a "topic" sentence. It is relatively easy to construct systematic summaries of such books.

Important points of technique are:

(1) Don't make any notes until you have read each section or paragraph through as a whole.
(2) Use your own words and phrases, rather than slavishly copying out of the book, but make sure that the meaning is accurately reproduced.

Use of Cards

When you have an essay to write or a special subject to investigate, you will have to find out all you can of what others have written on the topic. You need some handy way of recording and assembling the relevant information. For some purposes it may be enough simply to record the page numbers of textbooks on which you can find information. Some students are very good at supplying references on particular topics, and are virtually "walking libraries". Their skill results from wide reading and an orderly and retentive memory, but they also use mechanical aids—usually a card index of some sort.

In approaching the intensive study of a particular topic, you probably have no clear idea of how you are going to treat it, nor of the relevance of each piece of information as it comes to hand. Therefore you need to record each piece of information separately, so that you can eventually shuffle your notes into any sequence that will suit your purpose. The best way of doing this is to make your notes on cards. These are cheap, and available at any stationers in standard sizes, 3 × 5 inches or 4 × 6 inches. Put down the source of each note in standard form at the top of the card, followed by a brief summary of the section or article. When you have finished your researches, it is then easy to classify and label the cards, and to make cross-comparisons. Bibliographies can also be easily listed in alphabetical order.

Summary

It is essential to take notes. You should think carefully about the kinds of notebooks and filing systems that are available. Some kind of loose-leaf system is best, together with appropriate files, folders and binders.

In lectures make sure that you sit where you can see and hear the lecturer without difficulty. Fairly full outline notes are usually desirable, particularly in factual lectures. Outline notes are more readily organized and memorized than pages of unbroken script.

You should review and fill in your notes on the same day. A scheme for assessing and improving your notes is described which involves the collaboration of two or three other students.

For further reading:
Bird, C. and Bird, D. M. *Learning More by Effective Study*, Appleton-Century-Crofts, New York, 1945.

CHAPTER SEVEN

EXAMINATIONS

One ounce of good nervous tone in an examination is worth many pounds of anxious study for it in advance. If you want really to do your best in an examination, fling away the books the day before, say to yourself, "I won't waste another minute on this miserable thing, and I don't care an iota whether I succeed or not." Say this sincerely, and feel it, and go out and play, or go to bed and sleep, and I am sure the results next day will encourage you to use the method permanently.

WILLIAM JAMES

EXAMINATIONS are intended to measure how effectively you have studied a subject, so the best way of preparing for examinations is to develop systematic habits of study. If you follow the advice which has already been given about methods of planning, taking notes, and learning effectively, you should have no difficulty with examinations.

There is no way of passing an examination without doing the requisite work for it. But you can ensure that you are at peak efficiency for an important examination. This means having a thorough knowledge of your subject and having it so well organized and understood that you can write about it from many points of view. It also means being reasonably calm and confident, and not fatigued or overanxious.

Taking these things for granted, you can improve your performance still more by (1) careful preparation and (2) skill in examination techniques.

Preparing for Examinations

The first preparation for an important examination begins at the very outset of the course. You should get a copy of the syllabus, if a syllabus is available, and make sure you know what ground has to be covered. Compare your textbooks with the syllabus, and make sure that they cover the ground adequately. Get from your teachers an outline of their courses together with book lists and important references.

Sometimes, as a matter of policy, no syllabus is published. Students are expected to be able to deal with all matters falling within the general confines of their subject. In this case it may be as well to go over the examination papers which have been set in the last three or four years and to make a list of the topics on which questions have been set. Don't rely too much on this information, however. Sometimes new examiners may be appointed who bring a "new look" to the subject and to the questions. Some subjects, particularly in the sciences, may be in a state of rapid change which may be reflected in the examination papers.

You should certainly find out all you can about the conditions of the examination; how many essays you have to write, how long each paper is, how many questions you have to answer, and what choice of questions is usually given; also on what basis marks are allocated—whether each question or section is equally weighted, or whether more marks are given for some parts than for others.

Teachers understandably deplore the "mark-grubbing" towards which my remarks seem to be tending. Examinations should not interfere with the ordinary course of learning, nor the treatment of a subject be distorted by the examination. In a competitive examination, however, you have to be concerned with getting as high a mark as possible. The ordinary term or class examination tends to be more of the pass-fail variety, and not to entail much special preparation. In final examinations, in which the students are classed or placed in a rank order, it is usually desirable to carry out some six to eight weeks of review, and to make a close study of the examination itself.

Review

As a major examination draws near, the student's problem is to distribute his time in such a way that study does not become a hectic fatiguing rush to deal with a great amount of material at the last minute. The sheer amount that has to be learnt necessitates regular work over the whole period, together with a period of some weeks' final review.

Certain principles are helpful in deciding at what times and how often you should carry out reviews in the course of the year. One of the most practical results of memory experiments is that material that has to be retained over long periods should be studied and restudied. Forgetting is made less and less rapid by repeated learning of the same material (Fig. 13). The diagram shows the number of repetitions required to relearn some stanzas of poetry on successive days. Memory traces become sharper with each repeti-

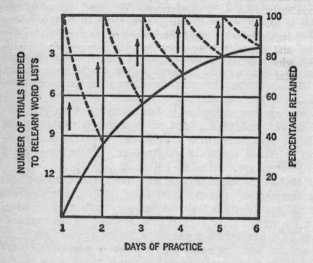

Fig. 13. Daily relearning of word lists. On each day the lists were recited to the point of one perfect recitation. Dotted lines represent curves of forgetting. The vertical lines with the arrows represent the number of trials required to relearn.

tion. Material which has already been gone over a number of times needs very little review to restore it to the level of 100 per cent retention. It follows from this that the more reviews that you do in the course of the year, the more easily you can perfect your knowledge at examination time.

The great advantage of learning by understanding rather

than learning by rote has already been stressed. Theoretically, you do not forget what has been understood and organized in terms of general principles. But often it is only by constant repetition that insights are gained, particularly in difficult subjects. Able students continuously go back over their work, think about it and integrate it. One of the benefits of taking examinations is in fact that you are forced to review previous work, to work in larger units than you normally do, to take wider views and to perceive the relationships of the parts to the whole.

Research shows that fairly frequent reviews, tests and examinations improve performance in final examinations. This is partly because frequent tests force students to work more regularly and spread their work more evenly over the year, and partly because much less effort is required to relearn what has already been reviewed.

So unless already provided for in the shape of tests and term examinations, some intermediate reviews are desirable

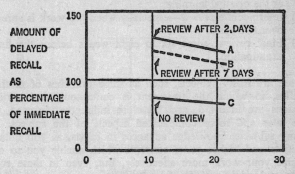

Fig. 14. Amounts of a historical passage recalled after 10 days and after 21 days, under three conditions: (A) review after 2 days (B) review after 7 days and (C) no review

between original learning and final review. Review is probably most effective either (a) soon after the original learning or (b) not long before the examination itself, the research evidence suggesting that (a) is more effective. At least this is known to be true over fairly short periods (Fig. 14).

Over longer periods the effectiveness of review is a joint

function of the distance in time from the original learning and the distance in time from the final reproduction: that is, review at a time equidistant between original learning and final reproduction will be less effective than either early or late review, although of course still much more effective than no review at all. Early review halts the early steep fall in the curve of forgetting: and when material is fresh in your mind you can run over it again more quickly and with less effort than if you leave it until it is half forgotten. Review before examinations revives and strengthens memories just before they are needed.

If you are to be examined on the work of the previous year or of the previous two years, a continuous process of review and consolidation is desirable. There are four steps in such long-term learning and retention:

(1) The original learning.
(2) Early review—on the same day or within a few days of the original learning.
(3) Intermediate review—especially when the work is spread over two years.
(4) Final review, some six to eight weeks before the final examination.

There are many subjects, such as some branches of mathematics, in which the treatment is continuous, and earlier notions are involved, and therefore indirectly reviewed, in the later and more complicated aspects of the subject. In many subjects, knowledge advances in bursts, as you obtain insights and higher order concepts which enable you to organize your work more effectively. But, even in these subjects, systematic periods of intermediate review are desirable.

The most common fault is to omit steps (2) and (3) above (and sometimes indeed to omit step (1)). When the original learning is imperfect, and is never consolidated by subsequent reviewing, the result is a hectic period of "cramming" before examinations. The common practice of cramming on the night before examinations may generate some memory traces which are fresh the next day. But it usually means a last despairing effort to tackle the work which should have been done long before. Cramming is likely to confuse the student, to dishearten him, and to leave him tired and below par on the day of the examination itself. And even if cramming enables the student to pass the examination, much of what he learns is very quickly forgotten and unlikely to be retained in the long run.

Review on the night before an examination should be quite a different thing. If you have worked systematically throughout the year your final review should not need to be more than one or two hours in order to revive and strengthen your impressions. But this limited amount of last-minute review should not be omitted. You probably do not need to be told this, but occasionally students are advised to relax completely before examinations and to do no work at all. The research evidence suggests that even the student who is already well prepared benefits from an hour's review just before the examination. There are some who even get up at 5 a.m. on the morning of an examination so as to perfect their detailed knowledge of some topic. But the usual advice, at any rate before a three-hour written examination, is to adhere to normal routine so as to be in the pink of condition in the examination room.

Methods of Review

In your review you should not need to reread your textbooks extensively. Rereading should be kept to a minimum. This is why a set of well-kept notes is so useful: instead of having to cover hundreds of pages of text you should have an outline in your notebook. Of course you may, in your final review, find some exciting new book which gives new and helpful facts and principles. But unless it is absolutely relevant to your purposes, it is probably as well not to try to master much new material in the final review, particularly if it necessitates a reorganization of your knowledge.

Recitation is effective because it resembles the activity of the examination room—recall without any direct stimulation from books or notes. After going over each section of your notes, set them aside and try and recall what you have been reading. Then check your recall against the notes. Any such active method of learning is better than mere passive reading of the notes.

In the same way that you give point to your work in SQ3R by asking questions, so in review you should try and predict examination questions. Ask yourself as you go through your notes, what sort of questions might be set on the various topics.

This does not mean going through old examination papers

and listing likely questions and their probability of occurrence. It is of course no secret that it is possible to predict questions by attending closely to hints dropped by teachers and professors. If a good deal of time has been devoted to a topic, or it has been given particular emphasis, you may guess that it will appear on the examination paper. Sometimes it will, but often it will not. It is rather doubtful whether intensive attempts at question prediction can ever be successful. But whenever any situation in human affairs is surrounded by uncertainty and anxiety, there are always some who will grasp at any straw.

Some "cramming" institutions actually list the probability of occurrence of various questions. In any examination there is in fact a limited number of topics on which questions can be asked. By studying the cycles and sequences of questions in old examination papers students sometimes think they can out-guess the examiners. But, with examinations, the past is not a good guarantee for the future, and you would be very unwise to rely too much on predictions from old papers. Examiners usually are not very much concerned about the relation of the current paper to those of past years. They are much more concerned to set a paper which is representative of the syllabus, and which can be tackled by the average student with a fair prospect of success.

How thoroughly you decide to cover the syllabus may depend in part on whether a wide choice of questions is given. If no choice is allowed you must omit nothing. If you only have to do half the questions on the paper it is reasonable to make a special study of those parts of the subject that interest you. But do not conclude that since you only have to do half the questions on the paper you need only cover half the syllabus.

Old papers are best used to provide practice in answering questions. To some extent writing examination answers is a learned skill, and as such, needs practice. Rather than merely glancing over old papers and saying to yourself "I could do 1, 3, 4 and 6, but not 2 or 5", you should work out some of the answers, at least in note form: that is, take sample questions and list the points that should be included in a good answer. Show your efforts to other students and discuss the question with them. If you think that you need practice in writing answers in full, take one or two questions and tackle them as you would in the examination proper.

Working old papers also enables you to form a truer

assessment of what you do know and what you don't. Research shows that in essay-type examinations where there is a choice of questions, students do not always select those questions which they can do best: not having been put to the test, they do not know accurately their own strengths and weaknesses. Actual practice at writing answers gives more objective information.

You should make a careful schedule for your final review. The review for each subject should be divided up and assigned to a number of sessions, which should be well spaced out. Spacing out the review sessions is useful because it gives practice in recall: at the beginning of each session there will be recall of what was done at the previous session. Then you should include some time near the examination itself for an overall comprehensive review of each subject.

It is worth making a special effort to get the bulk of your review completed about a week before the examinations commence. You can then devote the last few days to quick, summary refreshers. There should be no last-minute rush nor late-night sittings drinking strong coffee and wearing wet towels round the head. It is always a mistake to try and ingest a great quantity of material at this stage. If you *have* got behind with your work it is usually better to concentrate on essentials, and to make sure you fully understand at least some of the groundwork, rather than to attempt to master the whole and to be left with a confused and only partially understood mass of ideas.

Avoiding Anxiety

A mild degree of stress enhances performance, but a high degree of stress and anxiety is disruptive, and interferes with performance. This is true of many activities such as running a race, making a public speech, solving a problem or taking an examination. A certain amount of anxiety prior to examinations is a desirable spur to effort. But when the anxiety becomes excessive and is not channelled into productive work, it leads to a general inhibition of mental processes.

You may feel that this is a subject on which it is not very practicable to give advice. It is all very well to tell people to try and be relaxed and confident, but the advice is not often effective. Let us consider, however, the causes of anxiety. Anxiety stems from the fear of failure. Often there will be good grounds for this fear, when the student has done little work and realizes, too late, that the day of reckoning is at hand. The remedy for this kind of objectively based anxiety is obviously regular work and adequate preparation.

High anxiety does afflict others, however, when there appears to be no real grounds for it. In these cases it usually results from the conflict between a high level of drive or aspiration and the fear of failure, or of not attaining the high, self-set, goal. In the same way that a bicycle chain can be too taut so the level of motivation can be too high. It can be too high, particularly, for complex and difficult tasks, such as examinations are. High motivation speeds performance on an easy and simple task. But in a difficult task, where alternative methods of attack are possible, careful and systematic exploration of the problem is required. The excessively motivated person acts too impulsively and then becomes confused when he sees he has gone wrong. As the excessive motivation interferes with performance, the student becomes aware of this, worries about it, and anxiety builds up in a cumulative fashion. An excessive drive level makes for rigid and inefficient problem-solving. Try the following little experiment with a series of problems.

In each problem there are three water jars, a, b, and c, of varying sizes, and an unlimited supply of water. The problem is to arrive at exactly the specified quantity of water by manipulating the three jars.

	a	b	c	to get
1.	20	8	100	52
2.	3	5	18	7
3.	12	7	42	11
4.	31	12	154	123

The first three problems constitute a practice set, and all are soluble by the formula $c-b-2a$. The fourth problem, however, cannot be solved by this formula, or by any combination of the three jars, but quite simply by $c-a$. The first three problems thus give a "set" which is actually a hindrance in solving problem 4.

Try the problems out on a friend, and create as high a level of motivation as you can. Tell him it is an intelligence test, that he is to work as fast as possible, and that you will time him in seconds on each problem. These conditions nearly always make problem 4 difficult or even insoluble, because the subject is working under stress, and in his hurry, misses the simple solution.

Similarly, in examinations, questions can be misread, and obvious solutions overlooked because the student is too eager and in too much of a hurry to give them careful thought.

The best way of avoiding stress is to leave time for exercise, sport and recreation, to discuss your work with others, and generally to lead a normal life. Anxiety tends to be worst in those who shut themselves away from social contacts and try and study all day and most of the night. There is nothing like an afternoon's sport or physical activity, in the presence of congenial companions, for getting a more relaxed and balanced view of work and its problems.

The other line of attack on anxiety is to generate confidence in your ability to cope with examinations. This is partly a matter of familiarity with examinations and prior success in them, and partly a matter of having a plan of attack. In war, and in emergencies, those who know what to do and have a definite task to perform seldom panic or lose their heads. Similarly if you are systematically working with a program of review, confidence should be generated as you make progress. A chart of your progress towards the goal should supply you with grounds for rational self-confidence.

Examination Technique—Essay-type Examinations

Much of the advice that follows may seem elementary to those who already have extensive experience with examinations. These points of technique are important, however, and even if you have already been well trained in taking examinations you may benefit from glancing through the following ten recommendations, and comparing them with your own experience.

(1) First, you should get a normal night's sleep before the examination. There are always some students who will brag that if they had not worked until the early hours of the morning they would not have been able to answer some of the questions. No doubt this sometimes happens, but often the answers produced by such students are muddled and irrelevant. It is better to have a clear head than a few extra facts got up the night before.

Get ready the night before the materials you will need in the examination room—pens, ink, a watch, and any instruments, tables etc., you may be allowed to take in.

(2) When you get in the examination room read the whole paper through carefully, noting all the instructions given about the number and choice of questions, alternatives, etc.

The first sight of the paper is always a little disconcerting, even to those who are well prepared. Some questions which had been confidently expected will nowhere appear, while some that do appear may seem impossibly difficult. Therefore it is as well to take a little time to consider the paper as a whole before developing your plan of attack.

(3) The next step is to make a rough time budget. Note whether all questions carry equal weight and decide how long you should give to each question.

(4) If you have a choice of questions, select and mark those questions you feel quite sure that you can do. This seems obvious advice, but students sometimes tackle questions because they seem to be important, or because they seem difficult. They think that the examiner will be impressed by their efforts to deal with a difficult question. This is nearly always a mistake. It is better to attempt the easy questions, in which you are not likely to make errors, than to tackle difficult questions because you think they will give you a chance to shine.

(5) Before you start on any particular question read it through very carefully, and make quite sure that you interpret the question correctly. Look for the "key" words in each question such as "discuss", "summarize", "compare", "outline", and make sure that you know exactly what the wording means.

Some of the terms which are frequently used in questions are listed below. Make sure that you are quite clear about the precise meaning of each of them:

Compare
Look for similarities and differences between.

Contrast
Set in opposition in order to bring out differences.

Criticize
Give your judgment about the merit of theories or opin-

ions or about the truth of facts, and back your judgment by a discussion of the evidence.

Define
Set down the precise meaning of a word or phrase. Show that the distinctions implied in the definition are necessary.

Describe
Give a detailed or graphic account of.

Discuss
Investigate or examine by argument, sift and debate, giving reasons pro and con.

Evaluate
Make an appraisal of the worth of something, in the light of its truth or utility; include to a lesser degree your personal opinion.

Explain
To make plain, to interpret, and to account for.

Illustrate
Use a figure or diagram to explain or clarify, *or* make clear by the use of concrete examples.

Interpret
Expound the meaning of; make clear and explicit; usually giving your own judgment also.

Justify
Show adequate grounds for decisions or conclusions.

Outline
Give the main features or general principles of a subject, omitting minor details, and emphasizing structure and arrangement.

Relate
(a) To narrate. More usually, in examinations:
(b) Show how things are connected to each other, and to what extent they are alike, or affect each other.

Review
To make a survey of, examining the subject critically.

State
Present in brief, clear, form.

Summarize
Give a concise account of the chief points or substance of a matter, omitting details and examples.

Trace
Follow the development or history of a topic from some point of origin.

(This list is adapted from that given by Bird, C. and Bird, D. M., *Learning More Effective Study*, New York. Appleton-Century-Crofts 1945, pp. 195–8.)

(6) In essay-type examinations make an outline of the main points you intend to include in each answer. If you start writing down the first idea that comes in your head and then continue with whatever ideas come to mind next, your answer is likely to be too disorganized. Without an outline you are likely to write off the point, or to forget to work in some of the important points in their natural place. Examiners tend to become impatient with long rambling accounts, and to welcome clear well-organized answers.

(7) Avoid writing at *excessive* length on the easy questions that you know a great deal about. There is, of course, a correlation between the length of answer and the mark awarded. But don't be "carried away" so that you write at unnecessary length. Keep the wording of the question always in your mind, and don't include irrelevancies. You must edit your material and select what is relevant from your available fund of knowledge. As much as 50 per cent of some students' answers would be better omitted.

Often the sort of introductory paragraph that some students write could be omitted. As part of the "warming-up" process, they include a few very general remarks, which may no doubt help them to get started on the answer proper, but are strictly a waste of time in an examination when you must to some extent be working against the clock.

(8) If you do write too much on some questions you will not have enough time for others. You should never do less than the required number of answers. If you can see that you are not going to have enough time to do all the questions, it is better to leave an answer unfinished and to go on to another, than to hand in less than the required number. If you find that you have no time to do the last question, at least write some notes about it in summary form.

The reason for this advice is that two half-answers will usually get a higher mark than one full answer, however well it is done. The overall grade is nearly always based on the straight arithmetic sum of the marks for each question, so that excellence in one answer cannot compensate for the omission of another.

(9) Try to write reasonably legibly throughout the examination. You are very likely to be penalized if the examiner has difficulty in deciphering your handwriting.

In a well-known experiment, the same examiners marked the same set of papers twice, once when they were difficult to read, and once when they were clearly written. Although they had been instructed not to be influenced by legibility, higher marks were in fact given to a paper when it was clearly legible than when it was not. Suggestions for improving your handwriting are given in Chapter 10. You will, of course, have to start practicing to write fast and legibly well before the time of the examination.

(10) Finally, leave time, if you can, to reread your paper before you hand it in. Many students do not bother to do this. If the examination has been something of an ordeal for them, they seem to want to escape from the examination room as soon as possible. Consider, however, that mistakes occur in everyone's writing. A negative may be omitted, making nonsense of a sentence. Plural nouns will be disgraced with singular verbs, and there will be often minor infelicities of expression which can easily be rectified on rereading.

Pay attention also to punctuation and spelling. Errors in spelling, in particular, always create a bad impression.

In mathematics papers more serious errors may be

detected, in computation, for example, or in copying out figures from the paper. In such subjects it is better to check each answer as it is done.

Making Use of Returned Papers

When examination papers are returned to you with the examiners' comments, you should try and learn all you can from them. Much can be learnt by correcting mistakes, and by putting out more effort where it is required. Yet many students, once the examination is over, seem to dismiss it from their minds, and think no more about it, particularly if they have not done well in it. By going through your paper carefully you should be able to see your errors of commission and omission. Your teachers may be prepared to outline to you the points which should have been covered in a good answer to a particular question. You can then ask yourself why you may have failed to produce such an answer yourself. It may have been the result of lack of knowledge, of interpreting the question wrongly, or just not recalling the right facts in the context of the question. By analysis of this sort, you may be able to diagnose faults in your methods of study and then proceed to remedy them.

Objective-type Examinations

In objective tests and examinations you are required to make brief specific responses only, such as underlining or encircling a word or symbol. Objective tests have some advantages over essay-type examinations. They can be scored without subjective judgments on the part of the instructor. They enable the subject matter to be fairly completely sampled, as a large number of items can be done in a short time. Their disadvantage is that they nearly always deal with specific facts, and do not demand that interrelation of facts which is a desirable part of all learning.

The main kinds of objective tests are:

I. *Recall Types*
   (a) Questions with a single correct answer
   (b) Completion exercises, when you have to supply the missing word or symbol to complete a sentence or proposition.

II. *Recognition Types*

(a) Multiple-response tests, in which you have to select the correct answer from a number of suggested answers.

(b) True-false tests, in which you have to mark statements true or false—a third category (doubtful) being sometimes included.

(c) Matching tests, in which you may be required to match such things as a column of authors with a column of book titles, or a column of dates with a column of events, etc.

(d) Other item types call for the systematic enumeration of facts, for definitions, for arrangement in order, etc.

The multiple-choice form is the most commonly used, so our discussion will deal chiefly with this form. Consider a simple example:

Robinson Crusoe was

(1) lost on an ocean
(2) left by his sailors
(3) lost in a desert
(4) shipwrecked on an island
(5) seized by bandits

Your have to check which of the five possible answers is right. If you know anything at all about Crusoe you will be able to rule out answers (3) and (5). And if you know his story at all you can probably eliminate answers (1) and (2), and select the correct answer, (4).

In the same way, in more difficult questions in which you may be unsure of the correct answer, you can usually eliminate the answers that are obviously incorrect, and concentrate on those that remain. In comparing the remaining possibilities, you will often have enough residual knowledge about them to make a good guess at the correct answer. For example here is a vocabulary test:

Circumspect means

(1) suspicious
(2) cautious
(3) investigate thoroughly
(4) act of circumcising
(5) mark out the boundaries

If you have met the word at all you can probably rule out (4) and (5). If you know it is an adjective you can eliminate (3). Only (1) and (2) remain, and comparing the two, you will probably "sense" that (2) is the correct answer. Logical elimination is of great help in multiple-choice items. Even when you don't know the right answer, you may know that four out of the five possible answers are incorrect, and thus be able to infer the correct answer.

Another common type of test is the true-false variety: For example—

5 centimeters is approximately 2 inches.   True/False

This item is an almost straight test of information. True, you will probably not store your information in this particular form. You may know that 1 inch = 2.5 cm. (approximately) in which case you can easily work out the correct answer. If you don't have this information you may be able to imagine what a centimeter looks like on a ruler, and what an inch looks like, and judge that the statement looks reasonable. But in many true/false items which deal with mathematics or physical science, you will find it hard to infer the answer if you do not know it. Of course if you guess at random you should get 50 per cent of true/false answers right—50 per cent is in fact the "zero" score in such a test.

Unless you are told in the test instructions not to guess at answers that you do not know, it will usually pay to guess. You will usually have some slight knowledge of the question which will make your guesses correct more often than chance. The scoring may include a formula to correct for guessing, normally

$$S = R - \frac{W}{(N-1)}$$

in which

    S = score
    R = number of answers right
    W = number of answers wrong
    N = the number of choices in each answer

In a true/false test for example, the score would be the number of rights minus the number of wrongs. In a multiple-choice test with five possible answers to each question it would be rights minus ¼ wrongs. But, even when these corrections are used, you should do better by guessing than by omitting questions, since your guesses are likely to be better than random guesses.

In statements outside the realm of mathematics and physical science, few general statements are true without exception. Therefore students learn to be chary about accepting as true statements which include such words as "all", "always", "never", or "no". In fact, such statements as "All leaders are tall" are very unlikely to be true, but at the same time there are plenty of general statements that are true such as:

"No mammals are born with six legs."

Preparing for Objective Examinations

In general the advice already given about preparing for essay-type examinations holds good for objective-type examinations also. Objective examinations seem easier than the essay-type because they involve recognition rather than reconstruction or the selective application of knowledge. But those who do well in the one type of examination usually do well in the other.

Since objective examinations often consist of as many as 100 questions they can cover the syllabus more fully than essay-type examinations. This means that you must cover the full syllabus in your preparation. In essay-type examinations, where a choice of questions is offered, it may be enough to make a thorough and detailed study of a few likely topics. In preparing for an objective examination the coverage has to be wider. And since you are likely to be asked for fact and detail, it is as well to read and reread your notes and textbooks many times, to ensure that you become wholly familiar with all the material.

Here is some standard advice about taking objective examinations. First read the instructions carefully before you start, and make sure that you follow them in detail. Note how many questions you have to do and make a rough time budget.

Before answering each question read it over carefully at least twice, and make sure that you have understood its meaning.

If you come to a difficult or puzzling question don't waste time on it, but leave it and go back to it later. Do all the easy questions first, and then go back to the others. Otherwise you may spend so much time on certain questions that you will not have enough time to complete the questions that you do know the answers to.

Unless you are told not to guess, you should guess at those answers of which you are unsure. And once you have made a guess you should not subsequently alter it. Research shows that first guesses are usually best.

The results of objective examinations should show you where weaknesses lie. The pattern of your wrong answers should tell you on which topics your knowledge is weak. You can then proceed to remedy the weaknesses.

Summary

Preparations for examinations should begin at the outset of a course of study, in the sense that you should study the syllabus you are required to cover and the kinds of examinations which you will have to take.

Fairly frequent tests and reviews are desirable. Little effort is required to relearn for an important examination what has already been gone over a number of times. To be most effective, review should follow closely on the original learning. For long-term retention intermediate periods of review are also desirable.

The final review preceding important examinations should be carefully planned to a schedule, to avoid any last-minute rush. Examination anxiety can be avoided by regular work, careful planning, and a normal routine which allows for exercise and recreation.

Ten points of examination technique are suggested.

CHAPTER EIGHT

THINKING

> If I have succeeded in my inquiries, more than
> others, I owe it less to any superior strength of
> mind, than to a habit of patient thinking.
>
> NEWTON

YOU may choose your life's work, your place of residence,
or your attitude toward the political issues of the day, either
by careful thought about the relevant facts, or by careless
decision, ignorant of the important facts. The same is true of
more minor issues such as what to wear, or what to eat or
how to cultivate your garden, or where to go on vacation.
Thoughtful people make their decisions after carefully assembling as much information as possible, checking its reli-
ability, using controlled imagination to draw inferences from
the information, and carefully weighing the probable consequences of the alternatives before them. Others make their
decisions impulsively on fragmentary information, hearsay,
or the unsupported advice of others. In many everyday matters, of course, the decisions may be of little consequence,
and there is seldom time to give lengthy thought to minor
issues. But study demands that you should be capable of
rational thought, and the "ability to think" is often given as
the main purpose of education.

This chapter is written in the belief that advice about
thinking and reasoning is both necessary and possible. It is
necessary because although everyone can "think" after a
fashion, much "thinking" is irrational, the irrationality of the
mass of the population being fostered by advertisers and
others for their own private gain. Everyone can be taught
to think better. At least he can be taught to define crucial
terms carefully and to think about their meaning, to assess
how reliable information is and how it has been derived, to
avoid wishful thinking, and to look for the hidden assump-

127

tions in arguments. Many of the other skills in thinking can only be learnt in specific subjects. Arithmetical reasoning can best be learnt by working problems in arithmetic. Reasoning about social issues can only be developed by studying the social sciences. Problems in chemistry or physics can only be tackled by those who are well versed in chemistry or physics. Really effective thinking and problem-solving presuppose not only possession of the relevant facts but a good understanding of them, and facility in their application and use. It is obvious that you cannot play chess or solve chess problems unless you are familiar with the moves and openings of the game. To think well you must have the information that the problem calls for, or know where to find it. But, assuming that you have the information, it is natural to look for general principles of thinking which can be applied to all kinds of problems. Training in handling words and numbers especially, is likely to help in many different sorts of problems because most problems can be reduced to verbal or mathematical form.

The Nature of Thinking

In much learning, excessive concern with conscious processes may actually be a handicap. This does not apply to thinking. Before you can improve your thinking you must observe and analyze your own thought processes. An account will first be given, therefore, of the nature of thinking, before any advice is given about techniques for the solution of problems.

In thinking there is some kind of representation of objects and events which are not immediately present to the senses. As a simple example, a child sees a toy placed under one of three boxes, and, after an interval, is told to find the toy. If he consistently chooses the right box the first time he must be aided by some kind of a "representation" or memory; in common speech we say he can remember under which of the three boxes he saw the toy placed. If he is able to talk, he may say to himself, "It's under the middle box," or he may have a visual image of the toy being placed under the middle box. This ability to think of objects and events in their absence is the first requisite of all the more complex forms of thinking.

The more complex forms of thinking are not very easy to observe by introspection. Most thinking involves imagery. If you think of what you had for breakfast this morning, you may have visual imagery of the meal on your plate, and also images of sounds, smells and tastes, together with some feelings about whether the breakfast was pleasant or not; or you may remember in more abstract and symbolic fashion, merely that you had "eggs". People differ in the vividness of their imagery and in the modality of the imagery. Sir Francis Galton, who first investigated individual differences in imagery, had strong visual imagery. He was astonished to find that many scientists seemed to employ no visual imagery at all. Those who have been long in intellectual work, may tend to think more in symbols and abstractions than in images of concrete things. Generally, we can say that the vehicles of thought are images, words and other symbols. Sometimes, however, thought seems to occur without much in the way of observable content at all.

Several kinds of thinking can be distinguished. In study we are naturally more concerned with reasoning and problem-solving than with "day-dreaming" and reverie. That is, we are interested in controlled and directed thinking rather than in free association.

The Development of Thinking

Thinking can be better understood by considering its development in children.

Thinking in the early years tends to be dominated by what is actually present to the senses. For example, a six-year-old puts the same number of beads into two beakers, A and B, which are identical in size and shape. If the beads in A are then emptied into a taller, thinner glass, he will say that the number of beads has changed because the container looks higher and thinner. Dominant perceptual features influence children's reasoning. That a quantity can stay unchanged in spite of differences in its appearance is something that has to be learnt. Similarly the adult notion that objects stay the same in spite of changes in their appearance, as they are seen at different times and from different angles, has to be learnt through lengthy experience. Many ideas which adults take for granted, ideas of causation, of time and of space and distance, are constructions which are, as it were, imposed on experience.

At the primary school stage thinking begins to overcome its dependence on concrete particular situations. Children can now manipulate ideas about objects, but only ideas about concrete objects, not about abstractions. Arithmetic operations, for example, are readily carried out with counters or concrete objects, but the same operations are not understood when they are presented in verbal or symbolic form.

Children are usually unable to manipulate ideas about ideas until they reach the age of eleven or twelve: it is only then that they become fully capable of forming abstract concepts, reversing temporal sequences in thought, and dealing with space, time and number as systems abstracted from sensory experience.

As thinking becomes more adult and more complicated, there is less and less reliance on directly observed events, and an increasing tendency toward abstraction.

Parallel with this tendency toward abstraction is a decrease in the motor activity which accompanies thought. Some not very intelligent individuals (and at times quite intelligent ones) can be heard to talk to themselves or to mutter their thoughts out loud, as though some activity of the speech mechanism is a necessary accompaniment of thought. When people are asked to imagine bending their right arm, small muscle potentials are actually produced in the right arm. When they are asked to imagine looking up at the Eiffel Tower recordings from the eye muscles resemble those actually made by moving the eyes upwards. In imagining rhythmic activities such as using a hammer, rhythmic bursts of nervous activity are produced. Such facts have suggested that thinking involves not only the brain but the whole body. Moreover, complete relaxation of the musculature results in cessation of all conscious mental activities. The actual bodily activity accompanying thought is important in children and in animals. Some dogs can make visual discriminations much better when they are free to move about than when they are still. This does not mean, however, that adult subjects need to be bodily active in order to think effectively. As thinking becomes more abstract and more symbolic, it becomes more purely a brain process in the mature person. The less intelligent show greater motor potentials during thought than more intelligent people.

The great advantage of thought is that it allows implicit manipulation of the environment. Moreover, it allows you to reverse natural sequences of events, or to deal with theoretical or even impossible events. It enables you to anticipate future events, and consequences. As an everyday example, suppose you get into your car, switch on the ignition, and the warning light and dashboard gauges do not work. Most drivers will infer at once that there is either a dead battery or a break in the electrical system. Suppose that the dashboard lights work, but that when the starter is operated no sound comes from the starter motor. This suggests that current is not getting through to the starter motor, and so on. Assuming that the driver has a little relevant knowledge, a rough map of the electrical system of the car, he can infer at once, by mentally going over or by mentally reversing the processes that normally occur in starting the car, where the fault is likely to be. True, there may be equally likely alternative explanations of the fault, and only actual trial will decide which is the correct explanation.

Elementary fault tracing of this kind supplies a useful model for a great deal of thinking and problem-solving. First the thinker must have a cognitive "map" or "model" to guide him in his thinking. Secondly, from his knowledge of what "ought to" happen, based on past observations, he can infer the probable cause of a difficulty and suggest remedies. But, thirdly, his deductions will have to be tested in practice, and often there will be no way of deciding between alternatives except by actual trial and error. Thought can save a great deal of trial and error—that is its main purpose—but actual practice and observation are also necessary to verify thinking. You should not regard thinking as mere contemplation. Often the best thinking accompanies activity and observation.

Concepts

All human thinking is based on concepts. A concept is defined as a common response (usually verbal) to a class of objects or events. Concepts are used at many levels of abstraction, from the simpler concepts of young children in naming and identifying common objects such as plates, dolls and bottles, to the highly abstract motives, such as "force" used by scientists. Before a concept can be formed there must be abstraction and generalization. As an example, a child of eighteen months may reach out for a burning candle, attracted by its brightness. On being burnt or mildly scorched, the child quickly withdraws his hand. If he is then confronted with a lighted electric bulb, a tentative movement to reach out and touch the bulb is likely to be quickly followed by a withdrawal movement. The identical element of "luminosity" has been abstracted from these two situations; the child has made the generalization that luminous objects burn, and withdraws his hand.

Here is a more complicated problem in abstraction and generalization for you to work out. What is it that the air-planes 1, 4 and 5 have in common, which the other air-planes do not have?

When you have noticed the common characteristics shared by 1, 4 and 5, you have in fact identified a class of aircraft, and could give it a name, and recognize fresh instances as either belonging to the class or not.

Classifying objects and events in this fashion serves to reduce the complexity of the environment. Once an object has been classified and labelled, further inferences can be made about it. A wriggling object about two feet long is seen to be a snake, and further, since it has a central zigzag

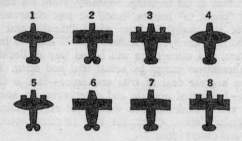

Fig. 15. Aircraft silhouettes

line down its back, it is inferred to be an adder and therefore poisonous. Similarly a man may be introduced to you as a teacher, and hence other properties which are associated with the class of teachers may be inferred, as that he is a sober responsible citizen, more concerned with social welfare than with making money, etc. There are thus two aspects of concept formation:

(1) An act of classification on the basis of observed prop-erties.
(2) A set of associations or inference as to unobserved prop-erties.

Objects are classed together because they are similar or have attributes in common. If you are to abstract the common elements, you must have experience of an array of instances which have some common and some different features. If one feature or element is common and recurrent, while others vary, the common element will tend to be noticed and abstracted. If you see a red lampstand, a red dress, and a red face in close juxtaposition, the common element of redness will tend to be abstracted. Generally if a property A occurs now with B, C, D, now with C, F, H, and again with E, G, B, the property A tends to be abstracted and recognized by itself, apart from particular bodies. In this way class concepts are formed—in the example above the concept of "redness".

The kinds of abstraction which are made are determined by language and culture. Indo-European languages embody concepts and abstractions of higher degree than those of more primitive languages.

"The class of prime numbers, animal species, the large range of colors included in the category 'blue', squares and circles: all of these are inventions. . . . They do not 'exist' in the environment. The objects of the environment provide the cues or features on which our grouping may be based, but they provide cues that could serve for many groupings other than the ones we make." *

The Development of Concepts

The process by which a young child acquires words and concepts was described by C. L. Hull as follows:

"A young child finds himself in a certain situation, reaches to it by approach, say, and hears it called 'dog'. After an indeterminate intervening period he finds himself in a somewhat different situation and hears that called 'dog'. . . . Thus the process continues. The 'dog' experiences appear at irregular intervals. The appearances are thus unanticipated. They appear with no obvious label as to their essential nature. This precipitates at each new appearance a more or less acute *problem* as to the proper reaction. . . . Meanwhile the intervals between the dog experiences are filled with all sorts of other absorbing experiences which are contributing to the formation of other concepts. At length the time arrives

* J. S. Bruner *et al*, *A Study of Thinking*. London, Chapman & Hall, 1957.

when the child has a 'meaning' for the word dog. Upon examination this meaning is found to be actually a characteristic more or less common to all dogs and not common to cats, dolls and teddy bears. But to the child the process of arriving at this meaning or concept has been largely unconscious." *

Thus when a child can name dogs accurately and distinguish them from non-dogs, he has attained the concept of "dog" and must be able to recognize the essential (defining) attributes which are constantly present along with varying concomitants. Luckily the child's task is made easier by redundancy in nature; dogs have many things in common —a tail, a hairy coat, a foul smell and a bark (as well as the filthy habits and abject fawning which characterize the species)—so that the possession of some of these attributes is a fair guarantee of the others being present also.

Meaningful and useful concepts can only be developed after experience of many instances of the class. Farmers for example can form some idea of the economic utility of a cow by observing the conformation of the udder. An experienced dairy farmer has developed the concept of a "good udder" from observation of many hundreds of cows.

Likewise professional wine-tasters develop remarkable discrimination in tasting wines, and have their own special vocabulary and concepts. If new concepts are to have meaning, experience of a considerable array of instances is usually required. This is one reason why practical work is so important in many subjects. The person who has made a wireless set is in a much better position to study electronics than someone who has not. Music cannot be studied intelligently by those who have never played a musical instrument. But mere experience is not enough. Explicit statements of principle are also required. This is more obviously true of concepts such as kilowatt, or motive, which are not directly observable. Here explicit verbal definition is required, and also appeal to relevant experience.

The Dangers of Categorization

Conceptual thinking reduces the complexity of the environment, enables objects to be identified, does away with the

* C. L. Hull, *Quantitative Aspects of the Evolution of Concepts.* Psychol. Monographs No. 123, 1920.

necessity for constant learning and provides a framework of categories for the ordering of objects and events. But the categories can become too rigid and can oversimplify experience. It has been shown, for example, that the racially prejudiced fail to observe individual differences amongst Negroes. Once a strange individual is classed as Negro or colored, further observation of him is impeded. Similarly young men may classify girls as pretty and not pretty, and fail to observe the eugenic characteristics which would provide a more serviceable classification. Concepts can actually be a hindrance to clear thinking. The traditional distinction between "spending" and "saving", for instance, can be too rigidly applied. Spending may be an investment when money is spent on education or health, and saving pointless if money is accumulated in a biscuit-tin until the death of the owner. Ordinary language makes us put things into separate categories, as clever or stupid, normal or abnormal, when the underlying attributes are spread out on a continuum which cannot properly be split into two separate categories.

Errors are made in the act of classification itself, but even more markedly in the inferences that are made about unobserved properties, on the basis of the classification. Once you have classed a person as bearded or a dog-lover or a member of the working class, a bluestocking or a supporter of the campaign for nuclear disarmament, you are likely to endow that person with other attributes which you know or believe to be associated with the class. This is going beyond the evidence, but life would be intolerably complicated if probable inferences were not made at every turn. In scientific thinking, on the other hand, you need to know precisely how much trust can be put in these inferences. For the sake of example someone might state that all who eat pudding with only a spoon are of plebeian origin. An empirical study might show:

	Eats pudding with spoon only	Eats pudding with spoon and fork	
Father employed in manual work	800	200	1,000
Father not employed in manual work	700	300	1,000
	1500	500	2,000

The association between the habit and plebeian origin would be so small, that you clearly would not be justified in making any inferences from one to the other.

In the inferences made in daily life precise information of this kind is seldom available, and you are seldom able to validate the inferences made: if you are a fisherman you may believe that the fish in a certain stream will rise to one type of fly more than to others. In fact the fish rise readily to almost any fly on some occasions, are more selective on others, and sometimes refuse to rise at all. The fisherman has no chance of making a controlled statistical study of how many fish will rise to various kinds of fly. But as he must use something, he will make probable inferences on necessarily inadequate experience. The same is true of all situations where the outcomes are influenced by many factors, but only one or two can be controlled. You decide that vitamin pills will do you good, or that a fertilizer will do your garden good, but are never able to isolate the effect of their treatments from the effects of other factors.

The point to remember is that the associations which are built up around your concepts are often based on inadequate evidence. The associations contained in many bits of folklore are patently untrue, as that country-dwellers are slow-minded, that professors are absentminded, that atheists are immoral, that alcohol is a stimulant, that lunatics are violent, etc. In the same way some of your more personal sets of associations may be mistaken. To think clearly, some dissociation of existing ideas may be necessary; the French writer Remy de Gourmont wrote a book advocating the dissociation of ideas.

Yet thought can only proceed because ideas are associated. The common associations which often determine the order of thoughts in idle reverie are not haphazard. The first ideas that come into most people's heads when confronted with the word "needle" are "thread" or "pins"; "hammer" suggests "nail", and "lamp" suggests "light"; "table" suggests "chair", etc. Certain associations are very common; they depend on verbal habits. Extending this observation from single words to more complex sequences of thought, much commonplace thinking falls into customary sequences and the stream of thought flows in well-worn channels. Conformity with conventional thought-patterns is often advantageous in passing the more elementary forms of examinations. A more critical attitude is required in many branches of higher learning.

Fallacies

The irrationality of everyday thinking has been much belabored, and with good reason. There is seldom time to achieve full analysis and description of everyday problems. Thinking often starts from vague or incorrect definitions of the problem, and proceeds with essential elements lost. In many daily activities there is no time to think: action is called for. There is no time for the diligent collection of evidence, sifting of arguments and balancing of rival testimonies that any complex decision really demands. Instead civilization advances by handing over its more complex thinking to special groups such as accountants, mathematicians and research workers.

The determining factors in everyday thinking are often subconscious. Most people could not put their thoughts and feelings into words, but are content to dismiss what they don't like as "bosh", "tripe", or "nonsense". Many feel or intuit the consequences of intended action, but can give no explicit formulation of the grounds of their feelings. Since the time of Machiavelli, many unscrupulous propagandists, including modern advertisers, have believed that nothing is to be gained by appealing to the intellect. And thinking is notoriously influenced by hopes, fears, and prejudices. On politics, religion and sex, rational discussion is always difficult because on these subjects everyone has established systems of belief which are associated with strong emotions.

It is less easy to detect fallacies in arguments which support your own views than in arguments which are in opposition to them. A "butter-bloc" senator is said to have argued:

In China people don't eat butter.
In China babies are born with slant eyes.
Do you want your children to have slant eyes?

This argument appears preposterous and absurd, but is no different in form from the common logical fallacy of the "undistributed middle":

All A is B.
All A is C.
All B is C.

Common habits of thought which you should be careful
not to carry over into academic work include:

(1) Selection of evidence to fit in with pre-existing ideas.
(2) Assuming that one event is the cause of another without adequate evidence.
(3) Overgeneralizing on the basis of small samples or
limited experience.

(i) Personal bias leads to the selective treatment of evidence, those facts which support a favored view being
stressed, but those which oppose it being ignored. If you
are attracted by a job, a political party or by someone
of the opposite sex, you inevitably tend to see all the
"pros" but to be blind to some of the "cons". In the
life of action and decision, of course, you cannot sit on
the fence endlessly weighing the pros and cons. A slightly
more favorable view of things than the facts really war-
rant supplies that enthusiasm without which nothing would
ever get done. But in study you must be more objective,
and pay special attention to the negative instances and
exceptions which upset all general statements. Many discoveries have been made when the research worker at-
tends to some awkward fact which is upsetting the beauti-
ful picture which he thinks he ought to be able to see.
(ii) Science proceeds by experiment. Typically before one
event can be said to be the cause of another there must
be an experiment of the type:

	Before treatment	After treatment
Experimental group	X_1	X_2
Control group	X'_1	X'_2

If the effects of any treatment are to be assessed there
should be an experimental group and a control, and measurements or observations both before and after treatment.
The difference $(X_1-X_2)=d$ is then compared with the
difference $(X'_1-X'_2)=d'$, and only if $(d-d')$ is of significant size can the effect of the treatment be assessed.
This is true if you are trying to assess the effect of a
teaching method in learning, the effect of an article of
diet on growth, the effect of changes in the law or the
frequency of murders etc. In everyday observations a control group is seldom available. Sometimes indeed only

one cell in the above table, X_2, is available. When some new educational measure is instituted, for example, interested parties will come out with the opinion that it is "working well", although they have no control group and no measure of initial performance. Reliance on opinion or authority is no substitute for evidence.

(iii) To give personal impressions the status of general laws is a natural tendency in human thinking, most obvious in those who are both sincere and narrow-minded. This is tantamount to drawing big conclusions from small samples, which everyone has to do in daily life. In academic work you must be more chary of doing so, and more aware of the complexities of nature.

Problem Solving

Problems are of many different kinds, including scientific problems dealing with explanations and discovery, and practical problems about what sort of action to take in everyday affairs. Some people are much more resourceful than others when confronted with a problem, not only because they are more intelligent but also because they adopt better procedures.

Most of the information on this topic comes from experiments in which the subjects have been told to think out loud while solving problems. Among the many experimental problems used have been mechanical puzzles, mathematical problems, problems involving the construction of apparatus, and a great number of puzzles and problems in verbal form. In this section we shall survey experiments using mechanical puzzles, apparatus problems, and abstract verbal problems. Laboratory problems differ from problems in everyday life in that the subject is usually given all the relevant information required, and the problem does admit a definite solution. In many everyday problems, on the other hand, you may not have all the necessary facts, and the problem may be insoluble.

In one series of experiments the subjects were given mechanical puzzles, such as two interlinked rings which had to be separated. Solution was first reached by random manipulation, the subject having little idea of how he reached it. But he noticed the place or part of the puzzle in which success was reached, and was able to use hindsight, that is to reverse the order of operations in thought, working back from the solution. Eventually he was able to analyze the successful procedure into a series of steps. The first attempts at analysis are perceptual, as the subject notices things while actually looking at the puzzle and manipulating it. In later analysis the subject can formulate the procedure in words, and understands the principle involved. When given other puzzles of the same general kind, nearly all improvement results from conscious analysis of the principles involved. In other words, a sudden "flash of insight" into a problem is not enough. It is necessary to go on and to formulate the solution precisely in words or symbols. Only when the solution has been precisely stated can it be verified or communicated to others. Suppose you are asked to prove that the opposite angles in diagram A are equal.*

Fig. 16. The problem is to prove that angles a and b are equal

If the angles are drawn in as in diagram B there is an immediate flash of insight. But the solution still needs to be formulated precisely:

$$a = 180° - c$$
$$b = 180° - c$$
$$\therefore a = b$$

The point is that, in thought, the solution is seen in an instant, because several relationships can be perceived almost simultaneously. But the language in which solutions must be encoded only allows of successive statements, so the elements of the solution must be sorted out and put into a sequence.

The importance of understanding preliminary instructions, avoiding false assumptions, and getting the right "direc-

* This illustration is taken from Miller, G. A., *Language and Communication*. McGraw-Hill, 1951, p. 235.

tion" were illustrated in an experiment by Maier.* His subjects were given four wooden rods, two lengths of wire, eight pieces of lead tubing, a C-clamp, two burette clamps, several pieces of chalk, and a heavy table which was not to be moved.

In addition there were the walls and low ceiling of the room.

The problem was to construct two pendulums, each of which would swing over a designated point on the floor, and so constructed that they would have a piece of chalk fastened to them which would mark the floor at the point designated.

The correct solution was to wedge a rod against the ceiling and hang the pendulum from the ends of the rod.

One group was given the problem with no additional instructions.

Another group was shown the component parts of the solution: how to make a plumb-line, how to make a long rod out of two shorter lengths and a clamp, and how to hold a rod against the vertical edge of a doorway by wedging another rod against it.

Another group was told that the problem would be simple if the pendulums could be hung from the ceiling.

A further group was given both the components of the solution and the hint about the ceiling.

In the fourth group eight out of twenty-two subjects solved the problem.

In the first three groups only one subject out of sixty-two was successful.

From these findings it appears:

(1) Knowledge of the component parts of a solution is not enough. The components have to be seen in their relationship to each other.
(2) There must be a correct "set" or direction to guide the attempts at solution, in this case the use of the ceiling. If subjects started off with the wrong direction, or made false assumptions, the problem became virtually insoluble.

Some experiments by Duncker * provide good examples

* Maier, N. R. F., "Reasoning in Humans," *Journals of Comparative Psychology*. 1930, 10, 115–143.

* Duncker, K., *On Problem-Solving*. Psychological Monographs, 58. No. 270, 1945.

of the processes involved in more complex and abstract problems. Duncker gave his subjects difficult technical problems in verbal form. One such problem was: "Given a human being with an inoperable stomach tumor, and rays which destroy organic tissue at sufficient intensity, by what procedure can one free him of the tumor by these rays and at the same time avoid destroying the healthy tissue which surrounds it?"

One subject reasoned as follows:

(1) Send rays through the esophagus. (2) Desensitize the healthy tissue by means of a chemical injection. (3) Expose the tumor by operating. (4) One ought to decrease the intensity of the rays on their way; for example—would this work?—turn the rays on at full strength only after the tumor has been reached. (5) One should swallow something inorganic (which could not allow passage of rays) to protect the healthy stomach walls. (6) Either the rays must enter the body or the tumor must come out. Perhaps one could alter the location of the tumor—but how? Through pressure? No. . . . (11) Adaptation of the healthy tissues by previous application of weak rays. (Experimenter: How can it be brought about that the rays destroy only the region of the tumor?) (12) I see no more than two possibilities: either to protect the body or to make the rays harmless. (Experimenter: How could one decrease the intensity of the rays *en route*?) (13) Somehow divert . . . diffuse rays . . . disperse . . . stop! Send a broad and weak bundle of rays through a lens in such a way that the tumor lies at the focal point and thus receives intensive radiation.

(The best solution is to cross several bundles of rays of low intensity at the site of the tumor.)

From such attempts at solution it can be concluded:

(1) The final solution is reached only after a series of intermediate attempted solutions, each attempted solution serving to reformulate the problem. When the subject thought "decrease the intensity of the rays on the way" the problem appeared in a new light and a new set of hypotheses was suggested.

(2) The ability to solve problems depends on the subject's ability to shift from one formulation of the problem to another.

(3) Solutions are transposable to a wide variety of other problems only if the subject understands the principles

involved. "Blind" solutions are restricted to the specific problems on which they happen to work.

(4) The solution was hindered because the subjects took for granted that they had to deal with a single bundle of rays of constant intensity, whereas the solution demanded a concentration of several bundles of weak intensity.

Summarizing the results of these three very different kinds of experiment, it can be said that:

(1) There is an initial period of exploration.

(2) The solution may be reached either by trial and error plus hindsight, as in the mechanical puzzles, or by successive reformulations of the problem as in Duncker's experiment.

(3) It is not enough to have the separate components of the solution available. They must be interpreted in the fashion that the problem demands.

(4) After a solution has been reached, it needs to be precisely formulated if it is to be fully understood and transposed to new problems.

Research on how college students set about solving problems in verbal forms revealed these differences between the successful and the unsuccessful:

Successful	Unsuccessful
Understand directions.	Misinterpret directions.
Choose a point of attack.	Confused approach to the problems.
Bring relevant knowledge to bear on the problem.	Unable to apply knowledge (although they often have the relevant knowledge).
Manipulate and reformulate the problem.	Failure to reformulate problem.
Carry their reasoning through to the conclusion.	Give up unless they can see the answer at once.
Objective attitude toward the problem.	Distracted by personal and emotional considerations.

The unsuccessful had difficulty in understanding the problem at the outset, were unable to reason systematically or to complete a chain of reasoning. Many of them did not believe in reasoning—either they knew the answer at once or they gave up. They had a subjective attitude toward the problems—that is, their beliefs interfered with logic.

In a wider context there are many factors which can impede discovery.

Hindrances to the solution of problems listed by Leeper * include:

(1) The separation in time of cause and effect—which hindered, for example, the discovery that mosquito bites were the cause of malaria.

(2) Perceptual incongruities or unexpected changes: for many centuries it was not realized that maggots turn into flies.

(3) Existing habits of thought may block solutions. Scientists were long in discovering that beri-beri was caused by vitamin deficiencies, because they were looking for bacteria as the probable cause.

(4) Interdependent causes: for example both calcium and vitamin D are necessary to prevent rickets.

(5) Intangibility or difficulty in observing causes, such as wind resistance to the speed of trains.

(6) Emotional factors, as when physicians refused to believe that childbed fever was transmitted by the physicians themselves.

Logic

Logic provides rules by which the truth or falsity of conclusions can be tested, but is not very helpful in the actual process of reasoning. Most reflective or critical thinking can be pictured as taking place in these steps:

1. Definition of the problem.
2. Formulation of hypotheses and possible solutions.
3. The search for evidence and relevant facts.
4. Drawing inferences from the facts.
5. Drawing conclusions and verifying them.

Logic is of some help with definitions, the rules of evidence and inference.

* Leeper, R., "Cognitive Processes", in Stevens, S. S., *Handbook of Experimental Psychology*. New York, Wiley, 1951.

Definitions

In study you are constantly advised to define your terms, and to make sure that you are quite clear about the meaning of the words that you use. In practice the meaning of words depends on their context, and it is not always helpful to give mere dictionary-derived synonyms. To define many words is often pedantic and unnecessary. The need for definition does arise:

(a) when a word has more than one meaning and is therefore ambiguous;
(b) when it only has a vague meaning, and greater precision is desirable;
(c) when you are using a word in an unusual sense, or inventing a new word as an abbreviatory convenience.

Perhaps the real point of definition is to make sure that you yourself know what your terms mean. It is easy to use such words as "income" or "adolescent" or "neurotic" without being very clear yourself what they mean.

Evidence

Questions about which facts and evidence cannot be assembled, such as the existence of God, are matters of belief, not matters of knowledge. But in all empirical work you must always be asking yourself "What are the facts?" Facts are obtained:

(a) through direct experience, that is, through the sense organs. Nearly everyone regards the evidence of his own eyes and ears as better than any other sort of evidence; yet the evidence of our senses is notoriously fallible—certainly witnesses invariably disagree in a court of law.
(b) by reading instruments of precision, such as rulers, thermometers, electric meters, speedometers etc., which may record variations and produce a continuous record.
(c) through experiment or controlled observation, as in most branches of science.
(d) from printed sources, such as textbooks, statistical reports, historical records, newspapers, etc.
(e) from other media such as radio and television.

(f) from other persons, who range all the way from competent witnesses to plain liars.

Printed sources are the main source of facts in study. Television is one of the major sources of facts in everyday life. Most textbooks are accurate and reliable, newspapers and television far less so. Popular newspapers distort the facts by selective treatment, and sometimes print statements in direct defiance of the facts.

Facts are strong when:

(a) Independent observers agree about them.
(b) The evidence on which they are based can be verified. Experimental findings, for example, should be capable of duplication by others.
(c) When many observations of the fact in question have been made.
(d) When the fact is in agreement with the general body of knowledge.

You should be aware that opinions and beliefs are poor substitutes for facts. The experience of a single individual, as represented in his beliefs and opinions, is often trivial as compared with the accumulated knowledge of mankind. Uneducated people tend to accept their personal experience as final, and resent any questioning of its adequacy.

Inference

Inference means going beyond a particular set of facts, and concluding that they imply other facts. When a wife sees lipstick on her husband's handkerchief, she will make certain inferences. When a motorist sees a patch of oil underneath his car, he infers that it is leaking from some part of his engine. A physician infers a disease from the patient's symptoms. This is the inductive "leap" from facts to their explanation, from the known to the unknown. As has already been described in the account of concepts, classifying by known properties enables further inference about unknown properties to be made.

The laws of logic are used to determine the validity of the inferences from given premises. A statement or proposition may be affirmative or negative and it may be an all-

or a some-statement. Thus there are four types of propositions:

(1) All X is Y.
(2) No X is Y.
(3) Some X is Y.
(4) Some X is not Y.

Many errors are committed in drawing inferences, because the ordinary speech used in these four types of statement is ambiguous. The diagrams of the Swiss mathematician Euler make this clear. These diagrams are based on the relations of inclusion and exclusion:

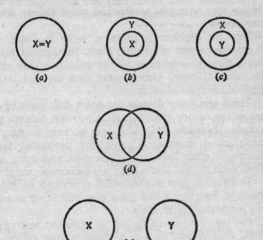

Fig. 17. Euler's Diagrams
a: X and Y coincide b: X is included in Y
c: Y is included in X d: X and Y overlap.
e: X and Y are mutually exclusive

If you think of the meaning of the four types of statement (1–4) you can see that type 2 unambiguously corresponds to diagram (e), but that type 1 could mean either diagram (a) or (b), type 3 could mean any one of the diagrams (b), (c), or (d) and type 4 could mean any one of diagrams (c), (d) or (e). This should serve to convince you that ordinary speech can hamper clear thinking, and that it may be necessary to use non-verbal symbols in order to think clearly.

Improving Your Thinking

The rather lengthy account of thinking and problem-solving that has been given so far may have left you in some doubt about how you can improve your own thinking. You can cultivate an attitude of thoughtfulness, but the general advice "Think!" is not very effective.

Here are some specific suggestions for improving thinking:

(1) Make sure that you understand quite clearly what the problem is.

(2) Where the problem is complex, write it down, or put it into some sort of graphic form. In complex problems the difficulty is to keep all the aspects of the problem in mind at once. Group your data so that it is not beyond the span of attention.

There are many devices for doing this, most of which are of the nature of visual aids. Counting, balance sheets, graphs, diagrams and check lists all help to summarize complicated material. In everyday problems involving choice, it often helps to list the pros and cons, and to give each factor some kind of numerical weight.

Translation into mathematical symbols is of great advantage, because of the great possibilities of manipulating mathematical symbols.

Putting the essentials of a problem into graphic form enables you to take a synoptic view of the problem instead of having to deal with each part successively.

(3) Look at problems from different angles, and actively try to manipulate the material. You should not become so fixated on any one attempted solution that you neglect other possibilities. You must be flexible in your thinking. The simple advice "Don't be blind!" is often effective, if it leads you to examine your assumptions.

Remember that habits of thought which have been successful in the past are sometimes a hindrance in new problems. Poor thinkers are typically rigid in their approach. So if one approach fails, get it completely out of your mind and look for a new method of attack.

Of course it is easy to say "Be flexible", but flexibility in thinking is not so easily attained. Sometimes it may help to drop the problem for a while, to talk to others about it, to go for a walk, drink coffee, etc., and then to return to work.

(4) If you try to anticipate the form of the solution, you may be able to narrow the range of possible solutions. If you ask yourself "What will the answer look like?", you will already have a goal at which to aim.

(5) Finally, remember that no problem can be solved without mastery of the relevant facts, skills and techniques. Lack of familiarity with the materials probably accounts for most failures.

Take an elementary problem like getting a nut, which has rusted on to a bolt, off the bolt—a problem which often defeats the amateur mechanic, but offers no difficulty to a trained mechanic. The trained mechanic will usually have a better and more varied assortment of spanners, and more confidence in his ability to shift the nut. In difficulty he will put penetrating oil on the bolt, or heat it up, or simply cut through the bolt with a hacksaw and use a new one. It is a problem which hardly generates thought at all in a skilled mechanic, because of his better armory of techniques.

In all specialized fields there are standard procedures for overcoming common difficulties, so that the necessity for thinking does not arise.

Creative Thinking

The combination of realistic and imaginative thinking is commonly referred to as creative thinking. Creative thinking occurs not only in the work of scientists and artists, but in everyday life whenever a problem arises for which there is no predetermined answer. Creative thinking can be involved in planting a garden, rebuilding a car, writing an essay, painting a picture, etc.

Graham Wallas singled out four stages of creative thought:

(1) Preparation (2) Incubation (3) Illumination (4) Verification.

In the first stage there is a period of initial exploration, when you find out all you can about the relevant facts, theories and techniques. The problem is defined and sharpened, but no further progress made. Next comes a stage of rest, when the problem is dismissed from your mind for a while. In the third stage, illumination, solutions may occur in a sudden and unexpected manner. Finally the solutions are worked over, criticized, and elaborated, and their correctness is checked. Further observations and experiments have shown that these stages do not occur in any clear-cut sequence. In most problems there is not a single "illumination" but a series of illuminations. It is true that these illuminations sometimes do occur at odd moments when no conscious effort is being given to the problem. But there is continuous interplay between the four stages.

Creative thought is hindered by rigid habits of thought and overconformity to established routines. It is often said, for example, that spontaneity is destroyed by overformal teaching in which proper forms and techniques are taught, but in which the student is seldom required to make discoveries himself or to develop his intellectual curiosity. Education which stresses the mere accumulation of information kills imagination and spontaneity. You should be aware of this danger, and ensure that you do not lose independence of thought by following your textbooks and your teachers' ideas too closely.

Summary

In early life thought tends to be dominated by what is immediately present to the senses. Later it becomes increasingly abstract and symbolic. There is a corresponding decrease in the motor activity accompanying thought.

For any sort of productive thinking a cognitive map or model is required, as well as observation, inference and the testing of deductions. The most effective thought is often not contemplative, but accompanies activity and experiment.

Concepts involve (1) an act of classification as to observed properties and (2) a set of associations as to unobserved properties. Experience of an array of instances is necessary if meaningful concepts are to be attained, together with explicit statements of principle.

Errors are often made in the act of classification, but even more markedly in making the unwarranted associations which occur in "stereotypes".

Everyday thinking is contaminated by emotion, by the selection of evidence to fit preconceived ideas, and by over-generalization from small samples and limited evidence.

From experiments on problem-solving it appears that the following steps are involved; initial exploration, successive reformulation of the problem, seeing the components of the solution in their proper relation, and precise formulation of the solution in symbols.

Logic helps in the definition of problems, in the sifting of evidence, and the drawing of inferences and conclusions.

From the practical point of view five general suggestions are made about how to improve problem-solving.

For further reading:
Burton, W. H., *et al.*, *Education for Effective Thinking*, Appleton-Century-Crofts, New York, 1960.

CHAPTER NINE

GROUP DISCUSSION AND GROUP WORK

Among the ordinary English . . . the habit of not speaking to others, nor much even to themselves, about the things in which they do feel interest, causes both their feelings and their intellectual faculties to remain undeveloped, reducing them, considered as spiritual beings, to a kind of negative existence.

J. S. MILL

STUDY is often thought of as a private activity: the learner shuts himself up with his books and masters the subject-matter alone: and it is true that the greater part of study is best carried out in this fashion. But books supply only the raw materials of learning. After facts have been taken in, they need to be interpreted, to be referred to previous knowledge, and to be reduced to order and system. In this process of organizing your knowledge, sifting it, seeing the parts in relation to the whole, and distinguishing the important from the unimportant, discussion with others is invaluable. Discussing your work with other students often helps to remove misconceptions, and frequently provides a solution to some nagging difficulty which has been holding you up. It can give you a fresh viewpoint and a fresh impetus to study. And the mere act of communicating and explaining your work to others can serve to clarify your own thoughts.

In the traditional "lesson" the teacher or lecturer speaks and the class listens. They talk back very little, and do not communicate with each other.

The diagram indicates that communication is all one-way,* and that there is a sharp distinction, indicated by the horizontal line, between teacher and students. Over-reliance on this method of instruction, although it enables students to pass examinations, tends to result in boredom and lack of interest. Information which is presented in too cut-and-dried a fashion allows no room for critical argument and discussion. It is the business of this chapter to set out methods of learning in which the learner has more scope for active participation. If you think that all that matters in learning is that you personally should work hard, and that your important relation is with your subject matter, not with your fellow students or teachers, you should remind yourself that

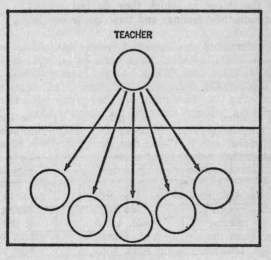

Fig. 18. Diagram of the social situation in the lecture

all learning in fact takes place in a social context. From childhood we have all become accustomed to learning from others and to imitating others. The very ideas that we have

* This analysis of learning situations is taken, by permission, from Oeser, O. A. (Ed.), *Teacher, Pupil and Task: Elements of Social Psychology Applied to Education.* London. Tavistock Publications Ltd., 1955.

built up about ourselves are largely the result of how other people have behaved towards us. We should learn very little in a condition of social isolation. You need only reflect on what it would be like to be on a desert island, or to be a member of some primitive tribe or, indeed, to be a member of a different social or occupational class, to realize that learning and motives for learning are closely determined by the standards and example of others. The ancient proverb says "Show me a man's companions and I will tell you what the man is." This is true, not only because we all tend to select as companions those who are somewhat like ourselves, but also because values, goals and working tempo are strongly influenced by the groups that we belong to.

The Effect of the Presence of Others on Work Output

As already stated in Chapter 3, when you are at work alongside others, speed of work tends to increase, at least in easy repetitive work. When the work is more difficult and more intellectually demanding, the presence of others may be distracting. But in simpler activities group work usually has a strong "pacing" effect on the slower workers.

In one experiment the subjects were required to put a stroke through the letters a, e and m, in a passage of prose,

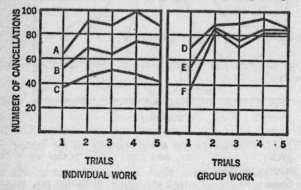

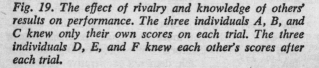

Fig. 19. *The effect of rivalry and knowledge of others' results on performance. The three individuals A, B, and C knew only their own scores on each trial. The three individuals D, E, and F knew each other's scores after each trial.*

working for five successive one-minute trials. Five subjects worked individually, adding up their score at the end of each work period. And five subjects worked in a group, their scores at the end of each work period being displayed on a blackboard. The graph (Fig. 19) presents the results obtained for the five individuals and for the group of five.

Note that although the individuals tended to improve their score with practice, there was more variation in their rate of work at the end of the experiment than at the beginning. The scores of the group, on the other hand, lie much closer together. After the first trial the slower workers all speeded up their rate of work so as to come up to the level of the others. In all trials after the first there is very little variation between individuals in rate of work. A group standard of performance was set up to which all the group members conformed. From this experiment you can see that the quantity of work done is influenced by the example and the known performance of others. This is a fairly general truth. If you work with a group of others whose work standards are high, social pressures will impel you to keep up with them. This is one reason why some colleges produce better results than others: they are able to maintain standards of work which influence all their students. One obvious way of maintaining your performance at a high level is to associate with others who also work hard.

The Advantages of Group Discussion and Group Work

Group discussion and group work are often to be preferred to private work.

(1) They stimulate motives and interests. Interest in work is more readily sustained by working and talking with others than by solitary work and meditation. This is true, although there are manifestly some individuals who prefer to work alone, and others who prefer to work with others.

(2) Some tasks are carried out more naturally and more efficiently by more than one person. Obvious examples are tasks such as carrying a ladder, checking a list, and a wide variety of everyday jobs. Here the cooperative effort of two or more individuals is much greater than their separate efforts would be. Possibly there are few study tasks which demand cooperative effort, but

in the laboratory or workshop small groups are usually more efficient than individuals. A division of labor allows each person to perform that part of the task for which he is best fitted.

(3) In study, group discussion is useful not so much as a method of solving problems as in enabling facts and theories to be brought into perspective. In some branches of higher study you may be confronted with very extensive reading lists, and a vast syllabus. You may be presented with more material than you can possibly learn. Your problem is to know which parts of the subject are of real importance, and to what depth and into what detail you should proceed. Unless you are able to distinguish the important from the unimportant, you may spend too much time on parts of the work that do not matter very much. Group discussion, with a teacher present, should help you to see which parts of the course are basic, and which are of only secondary importance.

Referring back to the division of learning into two stages, first the intake of information, and second its subsequent organization and use, we can say that group discussion is of most value at the second stage. Actual substance learning is usually best done alone, and there are other study tasks, such as writing reports and essays, where, although the individual can well take counsel in the planning stage, he must rely on his own judgment in the stage of execution.

(4) Group work and group discussion are desirable in themselves. All the world's work is done by cooperative effort, and consultation and discussion are part of the democratic way of life. Much research work, to take only one example, is now done in teams, many questions being too large for individuals to tackle alone. In group discussion we learn to accept criticism, and to become more tolerant and less extreme in our opinions. This does not mean of course that you always have to try and agree with others. Conflict and disagreement with others are often stimulating.

As mentioned in Chapter 4, there is an emotional component in learning. Group methods of work are of especial interest when the object is not only to transmit information, but also to influence the attitudes and motives of the participants. In certain areas, group work has come to be regarded as a method of "personality-adjustment".

Sociometry

Behavior in small groups has been intensively studied by the method of "sociometry". Sociometric tests are designed to study the network of friendships in a group. Each person is asked to state those he likes most and least—or those he would most like to work with. This provides a measure of the individual's acceptance or rejection by the other group members, and enables a picture of the friendship structure of the group to be put together. For example, in a group of six the friendship structure might be pictured like this, the arrows showing direction of choice.

Sociometry, which has become something of a cult, assumes that both the group and the individuals in it are most

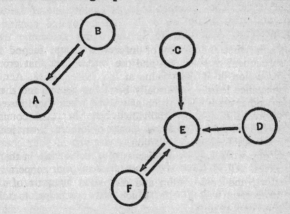

Fig. 20. The social structure of a group of six individuals. The arrows represent friendship choices.

effective when the members spontaneously accept each other as collaborators, and that therefore reciprocal acceptance and much social interaction are desirable in themselves.

Although many people would probably be more effective, both as people and as workers, if they were more sociable, research has shown that those who are the most popular are not always the best-adjusted nor the natural leaders of a group. Any individual who asserts himself tends to meet with some opposition and rejection; leaders have to be able to tolerate hostility.

The sociometric method, although it overemphasized the factor of mutual choice, led to much further research on groups. It led K. Lewin and his collaborators to their well-known experimental study of autocratic and democratic groups. They compared the behavior of boys and girls in artificially created democratic and autocratic atmospheres. In the democracy all policies were decided by group discussion and members were free to work with whomever they chose. In the autocracy the leader decided all policies and told each member what to do, and with whom to work. These different atmospheres produced very different behavior in the children. In the democracy spontaneous work groups formed, the children were cooperative and praised each other's efforts. In the autocracy the children were much more hostile and critical to each other, although submissive to the leader. They grouped together against one of the children and treated him so badly that he ceased coming to the meetings. According to Lewin, under autocratic treatment "a friendly, open and cooperative group, full of life, became within a short half-hour a rather apathetic-looking gathering without initiative".

Such experiments have emphasized the general truth that people are most interested in their work when they are consulted about it and actively participate in it, than when they are merely ordered to do things by others. You should, therefore, participate as actively as you can in your courses of study. If you look back on your schooldays and try and recall two or three vivid memories of your schoolwork, you will usually find that your most vivid memories are of occasions on which you were an active participator rather than a passive listener.

Progressive educators have for many years thought that education should be based on the interests and life experiences of the learner. In higher learning there have been efforts to get away from teacher-dominated methods such as the lecture, and to use more discussion and project methods.

Types of Discussion Groups

A common example is the practical class or science laboratory in which students usually work in small groups, may have to plan and design their own work, and are encouraged to discuss their problems together. Diagrammatically this situation is represented in Fig. 21.

There need be no status or authority barrier between teacher and student. The leader in his role as expert is freely consulted, but does not instruct the students in detail in what they are doing. The "social climate" is permissive and cooperative.

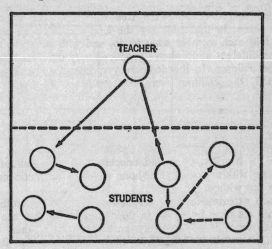

TEACHER

STUDENTS

Fig. 21. The social situation in a practical class or science laboratory

Another example is the seminar or discussion group (Fig. 22).

Here the teacher is present only in the role of a wise and experienced member of the group. Each person is free to contribute to the topic under discussion, and many of the usual restraints, which inhibit the expression of opinion in more formal classes, should disappear.

Many kinds of discussion groups may be used for different purposes.

(1) The lecture or *forum* which is just an ordinary lecture, but time is left at the end for the class to ask questions.
(2) The *lecture-discussion* includes perhaps thirty or forty minutes' lecture, followed by discussion. In the lecture

period knowledge is built up and the attention of the class directed to the topic. The ensuing discussion then serves to involve the audience more actively, often leading to more interest and better retention than the straight lecture.

(3) The *panel*, in which a group of experts discuss and debate a question, with some audience participation.

(4) The *directed discussion*, probably the most common form of discussion group in colleges and universities,

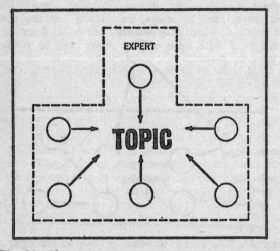

Fig. 22. The social situation in a seminar discussion

in which a teacher or leader is present in the role of expert, who has knowledge and authority not shared by the other group members.

(5) The *seminar* or round-table discussion, at which advanced students or research workers meet for mutual help and discussion. Usually such groups are small, and tend to be confined to those who are working on common problems.

(6) *Informal discussion* groups which tend to arise spontaneously in any student body in which there is a keen interest in the work.

Whatever you personally believe to be the merits of discussion classes—and some people who have been brought up on didactic methods are likely to go on preferring didactic methods—there is no doubt that they are more enjoyable than more formal methods, and should certainly find a place in most schemes of instruction.

Unfortunately they are not always used as fully as they might be, because they demand a high staff-student ratio, and cost more than lecture methods. But even if discussion classes are not adequately provided for you, you can still get together with other students to discuss your work. Most students naturally do discuss together some parts of their work, such as essays, translations and the problems and exercises which they are set. But to sit down to intellectual work with three or four others may be a novel experience for many.

First it may be as well to deal with possible difficulties. There are some who dislike any form of group work because they think that it brings into the open inequalities in ability. For no two people can talk together for five minutes without the superiority of one over the other becoming apparent, at least in such respects as verbal fluency and the ability to express ideas. But this does not matter, unless the participants are trying to compete with each other. The best discussions take place in a friendly permissive atmosphere, where the participants do not feel on trial. If some of them dislike each other they will tend to remain silent. There are many people who will refuse to speak, even among friends, if a stranger or some person that they dislike is also present. The presence of superiors similarly has an inhibiting effect on many: if they think their performance is being assessed by a superior they are afraid to speak. In organized discussions the result is often that a few "stars" tend to monopolize the discussion, while many are content to remain silent unknowns.

Discussion methods are of little use unless at least some of those present are reasonably well informed about the topic being discussed. There must be at least some present who can make statements that are based on evidence—otherwise the discussion may remain at the level of anecdote and unsupported opinion, and be no more instructive than an argument in a tavern. It follows that useful discussion is only obtained when the participants have put in some preparatory work and thinking.

Others who have tried informal group discussions complain that they often degenerate into trivial talk and gossip, and this is indeed more likely to happen when the participants are close friends. The remedy is to introduce some small note of formality into the proceedings. One speaker may take responsibility for opening the discussion, a chairman may be elected, visitors may be invited, etc.

Practical Rules for the Conduct of Discussion Groups

From the foregoing considerations a set of practical rules for the conduct of discussions can be deduced:

(1) First the group should be small enough to give everyone a chance to speak, but large enough to include a range and variety of knowledge and opinion. For most purposes there should be between four and eight members.

(2) In order to encourage free discussion the members should all be equal in status, and no one should be present who is in a position of power or authority over the others. The members should be reasonably friendly toward each other—at least there should be no sharp antagonism in the group.

(3) One or more members should take it in turn to open the discussion, but all must do some preparatory reading and thinking.

(4) The proceedings should not be too informal. A chairman should be elected to keep the discussion on the right lines.

Some students may feel that, in the absence of the teacher or expert, their knowledge is insufficient for any real progress to be made, but this attitude only reveals the overdependence on the authority of the teacher of which progressive educators rightly complain. At the very worst the group may come to realize that they do lack certain necessary information. But this realization should then lead them to take steps to get it, not to abandon the discussion.

To some extent the technique of group discussion has to be learned, and an effective discussion group does take some time to build up. The members must have time to get to know each other and to lose their first shyness. Those who have studied the behavior of small groups find that in time different "roles" arise. There is the "energizer", who impels the group into action, the "information-seeker", and the "information-giver", the "initiator-contributor", who puts forward new ideas, the "elaborator", who supplies examples and points out implications, the "opinion-giver" who states his own views of the question, and the "critic", who points out the flaws in what others say or assesses the value of others' contributions. Other roles are directed more to the maintenance of group solidarity. There is the "harmonizer", who attempts to reconcile disagreements, the "expediter", and the "encourager", who praises others' statements and states his agreement with them.*

These roles are not, of course, the monopoly of any one person. At times each person may take any one of them, but as a result of differences in knowledge and in personality, it is only to be expected that some will be more vocal than others. In a really effective group, however, there will be no silent members. A good chairman will see to it that at some stage each person is asked for his opinion, and will not allow the less capable members to be exposed to ridicule.

Problem-Solving by Groups and by Individuals

A consideration of the roles enumerated above should suggest to you that for some purposes, a group is likely to be more efficient than the same individuals working alone, for the individual working alone has to take all these roles himself. In many kinds of problem-solving, groups are superior to individuals. In one experiment, which contrasted the performance of groups of four and the performance of individuals, the problems were of this type: "On one side of a river are three wives and their husbands. All the men but none of the women can row. Get them across to the other side of the river by means of a boat which will carry only three at a time. No man will allow his wife to be in the presence of another man unless he is also there." (Counters to represent the husbands and wives were provided.) The groups took just as long as individuals to reach their solutions, but they produced a much higher percentage of correct solutions.

In solving problems, then, groups are more accurate than individuals. What are the reasons for this superior accuracy? First, groups not only make many more suggestions than individuals, but also are quicker to reject incorrect suggestions.

* Benne, K. D. and Sheats, P., "Functional Roles of Group Members", *Journal of Social Issues*, 1948, 4, 41–49.

They reject the incorrect ideas which escape the notice of individuals working alone. Most people are quicker to see flaws in others' suggestions than in their own. A group clearly supplies both a greater range of ideas and a greater range of critical viewpoints.

Often it seems that the mere knowledge that the judgment of others is very different from your own is sufficient to make you revise and improve your own judgments. In experimental problems, for example, such as guessing the number of beans in a bottle, or estimating the time interval between two taps upon a desk, individuals improve their judgments if they are informed of the full diversity of others' judgments, but not if they remain ignorant of how others differ from themselves. It is salutary to be confronted with judgments and opinions which are very different from your own.

Group work is likewise effective not only because of the wealth of suggestions put forward—it is not just a question of many heads being better than one—but because those members of the group who hold the more correct or accurate views have more confidence in their position, and are able to swing others round to it. The other members, if they are rational, will be prepared to accept others' views, and to revise their own, if it can be demonstrated to them, by logic or by evidence, that their previous views were wrong and others' views were right. In matters of opinion, on the other hand, when the question cannot be decided by logic or by evidence, there is a tendency for the majority opinion to carry the day, or for the members to be influenced by loyalties and friendships in giving their opinion or vote. Unless we have very strong views on a question there is a tendency to side with those with whom we are friends and to allow them to influence us.

This is a source of weakness in group discussion, and in committee work of all kinds. Some members may side with their friends when they have no very definite opinion of their own, or, when they judge that their private opinion is very different from that of the majority, they may keep silent from fear of giving offense or losing the good opinion of their friends. In the same way, subordinates are often unwilling to express their real opinions in the presence of their superiors if they think that their opinions will be unwelcome. That is why the best discussions take place among equals, and why a student discussion group can be more effective than an official seminar.

Summary

Group work is desirable in higher learning because it stimulates interest, helps to clarify ideas, and teaches individuals to cooperate.

Work output is influenced by the presence of others. Group work has a strong "pacing" effect on the slower workers. If you mean to work hard, you should associate with others who also work hard.

The various forms of group work lead to more active participation in study. Active participation not only generates interest, but leads to better long-term retention.

Several kinds of discussion groups are described and analyzed, and practical rules for the conduct of informal discussion groups are suggested.

In problem-solving, groups are more accurate than individuals because they make more suggestions, and are quicker to reject incorrect ideas. It is salutary for the individual to realize the diversity of others' judgments.

For further reading:

Oeser, O. A., *Teacher, Pupil and Task*, Tavistock Publications, London, 1955.
Strang, Ruth, *Group Work in Education*, Harper and Brothers, New York, 1958.

CHAPTER TEN

WRITING ENGLISH

Never write about any matter that you do not well understand.

COBBETT

TO be able to write clear and simple English is perhaps the most generally useful of all educational skills. Whatever your profession, you will need at some time to write reports, to present technical information or to compile statements and memoranda. The influence that you have in the world will depend very much on your ability to put your thoughts on paper. More immediately, in writing essays and examination answers, you need to be able to write clearly and intelligibly.

The purpose of this chapter is to suggest to you ways of improving your written English. It will deal with the choice of words, the construction of sentences, the linking of sentences into paragraphs, and the organization of ideas; and it will also include some hints on smaller matters such as spelling, punctuation and handwriting. It does not pretend to deal with writing of a literary or esthetic kind, but only with simple, functional English.

Before you can write you must have something to say, of course, and you must be able to impose some sort of order on your thoughts as you write. Crudely, the stages in writing are:

(1) You have certain ideas or facts in mind which you wish to communicate.
(2) These ideas have to be put into words and phrases, and written down.
(3) The words and phrases have to be run together into sentences, which must be grammatically correct and follow accepted usage.

(4) The sentences themselves must follow on naturally one from the other, mirroring the order of logical thought.

(5) As you write you must also keep in mind the impact that your writing is likely to have on those who will read it.

From this analysis it follows that faults in writing can arise at any or all of these stages. The author may be muddled in his own thoughts, or not have anything worth saying in the first place. His vocabulary may be inadequate for the expression of his thoughts. His sentences may puzzle the reader because they are badly constructed or defy accepted usage. The transition from one sentence to the next may be too abrupt, and the sequence of the argument may follow an illogical order. Lastly, the author may write at a level of abstraction inappropriate to his readers.

More positively, the analysis also suggests ways in which writing can be improved.

(1) You can attempt to clarify your thoughts before you start writing.

(2) You can enlarge your stock of words and phrases by reading good authors and newspapers of quality, and by engaging in talk and discussion of a more intellectual order than that which confines itself to sports, weather, and the price of things in the stores.

(3) You can familiarize yourself with grammar.

(4) Last, and most obviously, you can practice writing.

Enlarging your vocabulary

The *Oxford English Dictionary* contains about half a million words. The average college student can recognize about 150,000 words, but the number of words he actually uses in speech or in writing is, of course, much smaller. In telephone conversations only about 5,000 different words are used, and about half of colloquial speech is made up of clichés and ready-made phrases such as "How are you?" "Raining again!" "What's on T.V.?" etc. Thus a comparatively small number of words and phrases are used over and over again in ordinary everyday speech. This means that the actual speaking vocabulary of many people is small. This is most obvious in those who lead solitary lives. Henry Lawson has an amusing story about an Australian bushman, whose tongue has "got rusty", and who replies to everything that is said to him with "My oath!" Even in cities many people spend much of their time in commuting and in routine tasks which preclude conversation. The point is that in daily living it is possible to get by with a vocabulary limited to a few thousand words. The popular press and the organs of mass entertainment deliberately confine themselves to familiar words and to hackneyed phrases. So, if you wish to develop a more adequate vocabulary you will have to read more widely and converse more deeply than the general run of people.

The authors whose work is most admired for its plain and unadorned style include Swift, Defoe, Cobbett, Trollope in his nonfictional works, Samuel Butler and George Orwell. Most of them wrote rapidly and fluently without any self-consciousness about style, and without striving for effect. Much of the language of the older writers is archaic, however, and their subject matter of little interest today. You may find that it is worth trying to read them, in the hope that you may acquire some of their skill. But there may be little effect on your own writing unless you pay special attention to how their sentences are constructed and joined together. If your own written English is to benefit from your reading, you need to direct your attention to syntax, and probably to reread books several times. At the same time, everyone does pick up words and phrases from reading, and is unconsciously influenced in his own writing by what he has read. Those who have, over a period of years, read a great deal of good prose will develop a better vocabulary than those who read only tabloid newspapers and pulp novels.

The next step in improving your English is to master the essentials of grammar. Formal grammar is out of fashion, and is not much taught in schools. The chief argument against it is that it does not help *children* to improve their written English. "Grammar" and "composition" tended to be taught as separate subjects, and often there was little transfer between the two. Empirical studies on school children have led to the curious conclusion that learning grammar helps the learning of foreign languages, but not the writing of English.

The other arguments against grammar are that native speakers do not need it because they know without thinking, from long practice, what is correct and what is not; that grammar merely derives from the speech-habits of the previous generation and may be out of touch with current usage; that many eminent authors violate the grammarians' rules; and that it is based on artificial categories that suit Latin but not English. These objections to grammar really reduce to two: that it is too difficult and abstract for children to understand and use; and that, as traditionally taught, it is too formal and rigid. But neither of these is an argument against adults learning some of the more useful parts of grammar. Many good writers doubtless never had a lesson in formal grammar in their lives—but they might have been even better writers had they done so. And there is the striking example of Cobbett, who taught himself grammar with great labor, and then went on to become one of the most lucid of writers. There is no doubt that one important way of improving written English is to attend to grammar and syntax.

Grammar is outside the scope of this book. You should read such books as *The King's English* by H. W. and F. G. Fowler, or *Good English* by G. H. Vallins. The best English syntax, if you are prepared to take time to master the grammarians' terms, and are interested in the history of language, is still C. T. Onions' *Advanced English Syntax*.

The Choice of Words

Many authors say that you should not think too much of the words that you write. Cobbett wrote: "Never stop to make choice of words. Put down your thought in words just as they come. . . . Use the first words that occur to you, and never attempt to alter a thought: for, that which has come of itself into your mind is likely to pass into that of another more readily and with more effect than anything which you can, by reflection, invent." In similar vein Trollope wrote: "A man who thinks much of his words as he writes them will generally leave behind him work that smells of oil." Talented and experienced writers may be able to write quickly and fluently, without searching for words, but most of us find that our thoughts do not translate themselves into acceptable prose so readily.

Each person has several overlapping, but not identical, vocabularies. The scientist does not talk to his wife and children in the same words which he addresses to his colleagues. Each person, as he moves from place to place and from one group to another, learns a good deal of local idiom and slang, and something of the technical vocabulary of special groups such as engineers, sailors, farmers, etc. And on the continent of Europe it is not unusual to find people who talk Dutch at home, French at work and German to visitors.

You must not make indiscriminate use of these different vocabularies in your writing. In everyday conversation we overwork a small number of words which rightly find an important place in all speech and writing. But we also use a great deal of slang, colloquialisms, and stock phrases. These should not be used in academic writing, because they are usually inaccurate, and suggest a lack of thought and care on the part of the writer. In ordinary speech and conversation, clichés and familiar phrases have their place. At a noisy cocktail party, where silence is rude but conversation impossible to hear, communication has to be carried on in customary, prefabricated phrases, which have some chance of getting through the general din. Redundant words and repetition are often necessary in the interests of clarity. There is a limit to the amount of information that can be taken in in a given time. So in casual speech and writing the superfluous words are not altogether wasted. But in academic writing language has to be more accurate and more concise.

Exercises

(1) Compare the editorial from a popular newspaper with an editorial on the same subject from one of the "quality" newspapers, paying special attention to differences in vocabulary.
(2) Look up *jargon* and *cliché* in a good dictionary. Make a list of ten clichés. Political speeches, letters to local newspapers, and the sports pages of popular newspapers are good sources.

Use familiar words

As a general rule you should use short familiar words in preference to the long and unfamiliar. The Fowlers give these rules:

Prefer the familiar word to the far-fetched.
Prefer the concrete word to the abstract.
Prefer the single word to the circumlocution.
Prefer the short word to the long.
Prefer the Saxon word to the Romance.

As an example, the phrase "in the contemplated eventuality" is at once unfamiliar, abstract, circumlocutory, long and Latinized, as compared with "if so", which has all the opposite characteristics, more or less the same meaning, and more immediate intelligibility.

In fact, the five rules can be summarized in the first rule: prefer the familiar word. For the most commonly used words are short, concrete and of Anglo-Saxon derivation.

American social scientists have carried out empirical studies of the "readability" of prose. All their studies agree that short, familiar words make prose easy to read, and that long, unfamiliar words make it difficult. (The other factors which determine "readability" are sentence length and human interest.)

Sir Ernest Gowers in his *Plain Words* gives three rules which are in basic agreement with these empirical findings:

(1) Use no more words than are necessary to express your meaning. . . .
(2) Use familiar words rather than the far-fetched. . . .
(3) Use words, with a precise meaning . . . and, in particular, prefer concrete words to abstract. . . .

As a set of working rules, this advice is sound. Most people's writing would be easier read if it were put into more familiar, shorter and more concrete words. But different kinds of writing require different vocabularies. And a certain variety of words is necessary in all kinds of writing. Familiar words are not always adequate to express complex thoughts or subtle shades of meaning. There are always slight differences in the meaning of so-called synonymous words. There are supposed to be only two true synonyms in the English language: "furze" and "gorse". To take the argument to its extreme, it would obviously be ludicrous to attempt to rewrite the great works of English literature in the 850 words of basic English. It is said that in basic English "beefsteak" becomes "a cut from the back end of a male cow kept on the fire long enough". In the same way, too small a vocabulary leads to awkwardness, circumlocutions and inaccuracy. There is a context in which each one of the half million words in the dictionary would be the single best word to use. So, even when a short familiar word exists side by side with a longer, less familiar word, you should choose the longer word if it suits your meaning better.

"Readability", in fact, is a criterion more suited to advertising copywriters and to popular journalists than to more serious writers. Scientists, to take one example, could not write about their work at all if they were restricted to the use of familiar words, and any writer who used only the shortest possible words would produce very monotonous prose. In serious writing it is reasonable to assume that the reader is prepared to make some mental effort, but an increase in the size of vocabulary will always mean a decrease in the number of readers.

If you write on technical subjects you must use a technical vocabulary. People who have had a purely literary training are a little too ready to condemn specialist words as "jargon". Every department of science and every special subject have their own vocabularies, which the novice has to learn. The vocabularies are necessary not only to refer to objects and events which are unknown in ordinary discourse, such as "hydrogen-ion concentrations", but also because they stand for concepts which do not exist in ordinary everyday thinking. Of course, technical words such as "feedback" from electronics or "conditioning" from psychology, creep into everyday speech, and their originally precise meaning often becomes debased in the process. But learning a science is more than learning a technical vocabulary: it is also learning new ways of thinking; and scientific concepts are often enlightening when applied outside the special field in which they were first elaborated—particularly in the social sciences. Specialist words are therefore continually passing into common language.

Academic writers do have their own stock of vague phrases and circumlocutions, however, which can rightly be called "jargon". These phrases are centered round such blanket words as factors, situation, conditions, circumstances and relationships, and include such awkward expressions as "due to the fact that", "an important factor with regard to the influence of", "from the point of view of", "in so far as . . . is concerned" etc.

As an exercise, try rewriting these sentences in less clumsy English:

"To a great extent the conviction that we possess as to the permanence of objects is due to the fact that we perceive them in a stable relation to the spatial background."

"The question to be considered here is whether an infrahuman animal is able to abstract from a number of somewhat similar situations an element or several elements to which it will learn to make a reaction in such a way that if it is presented with a new situation containing these elements, it will react as it did in the training situations."

For many centuries there have been outcries against new words being introduced into the language and against others being overworked. Many writers have constructed an index of forbidden words. In the eighteenth century Swift condemned "sham", "banter", "mob" and "bully", and Johnson condemned "fun" and "stingy". Writing in 1878, Nichol protested against the use of "concept", "scientist", "fictional" and "recuperation". As all these words have now been accepted into the language, it is clear that such protests against the introduction of new words are made in vain.

But the case against overworking common words is stronger. Jacques Barzun's (1957) list of 50 forbidden words includes:

Jargon	*Feeble connectives*	*Affectations*
Basic	However	Devastating
Context	In view of	Formulate (=say)
Evaluate	While (apart from time relation)	Sensitive
Motivate	With (as a universal joint)	State (=say)

Advertisers' words	*Journalese and Textbookish*
Accent	Background
Angle	Crucial
Highlight	Emphasize
Pinpoint	Factors
Slant	Key (adjective)

These words, he says, are mostly good words which have been spoiled by careless or excessive use until they no longer mean much.

You may find it is worth constructing an *index expurgatorius* of your own. Constructing such a list of words and forbidding yourself to use them will force you to think about the meaning of words and should help you to develop more direct and accurate expressions.

The Construction of Sentences

A word standing alone has little meaning. The *Oxford Dictionary* lists 317 meanings of the word "take". The meaning of a word is variable, and depends on its context. We learn how words are put together from speech and writing, not from dictionaries.

The following rules about the construction of sentences are not meant to be too rigidly followed. They are meant to suggest a general pattern that you will adapt to your own purposes.

(1) In every sentence there ought to be one main assertion. Place the main thought in the main clause.

Two distinct assertions should form two separate sentences. They should not be needlessly joined together into one lengthy sentence by such connectives as "and", "or", etc.

Your sentences should never become so lengthy and involved that the reader loses his way in them.

(2) The normal order of a single English sentence is subject—verb—object or complement.

"The man drove the car too fast."

In a complex sentence the modifying or qualifying phrase regularly follows its subject:
Subject—modifying clause—verb—object.

"The man, who had just quarrelled with his wife, drove the car too fast."
Modifying clauses should, as a rule, follow straight after their subject, otherwise ambiguity may result.

"The room in the hotel which I preferred had already been taken."

In this sentence it is not clear whether it was the room or the hotel which was preferred. If it is the room which was preferred,

"In the hotel the room which I preferred . . ." would remove the ambiguity.

(3) Qualifying words such as adjectives or adverbs should be placed as near as possible to the words which they qualify. Adverbs and adverbial clauses can be moved about fairly freely, but often give rise to confusion. The rule is that adverbs should come if possible immediately *in front* of the word they qualify.

If you write:

"Girls are to appear on the sports ground only in running shoes",
someone will pretend that this means naked except for running shoes. ". . . only on the sports ground in running shoes" is clearer, or "The only place where girls

are allowed to wear running shoes is on the sports ground."

(4) You should never write a pronoun without considering to which noun it will appear to the reader to relate. In casual conversation you may say:

"Penrose beat Tal when he was world champion", but unless your hearer already knows that Tal, and not Penrose, was world chess champion, he may think that Penrose was the champion. Similarly in

"I have seen the advertisement for Nomalt's beer, but do not like it",

"it" is ambiguous.

You should repeat the subject of the sentence if the meaning requires it.

"He often writes to his old colleague who is now in Australia and sends him reports of his work."

This sentence should be rewritten either:

"He often writes to his old colleague, who is now in Australia, and he sends him reports of his work",

or

"He often writes to his old colleague who is now in Australia and who sends him reports of his work", depending on the meaning which you mean to convey.

Similarly you should repeat the principal verb, or substitute for it the appropriate form of the verb "do", where clearness demands it:

"The Americans distrust the Russians more than the British (do)."

(5) Prefer the active voice to the passive. "The dog bit the postman" is shorter and more direct than "The postman was bitten by the dog."

If you use many abstract and passive verbs your writing will lack force and vividness. Compare

"Consideration was given by the meeting to the question of the prohibition of stiletto heels,"

and

"The meeting considered whether to ban stiletto heels."

To prefer the active is the general rule, provided that you are saying that someone is doing something. If on the other hand you merely want to say that something is being done, the passive is more natural. "An election is being held," for example. Moreover, it is not easy to say that something is being done by people in general without using the passive. It is better to write "Hops are grown in Kent" than to manufacture a subject for the sentence and write: "The farmers grow hops in Kent."

(6) The first and the last words of a sentence get more attention than those in the middle. Therefore you should place the phrases that you wish to emphasize either at the beginning or at the end of the sentence.

This is a piece of general advice, of course, rather than a set rule. But you should be aware that if you write:

"Rules, as everyone knows, are made to be broken", there is less emphasis on the phrase "as everyone knows" than if you write:

"Rules are made to be broken, as everyone knows."

(7) Do not introduce too many qualifying phrases into a sentence. Academic writers tend to over-qualify their statements in their conscientious attempts to be accurate. Their sentences are full of such phrases as "usually," "to a certain extent," "under certain conditions," "other things being equal," etc. The excessive use of such phrases makes for a turgid style. Qualifications can be avoided by avoiding afterthoughts and by trusting to the general good sense of the reader.

(8) The more briefly a thought is expressed the more clearly it is conveyed. Sentences should be free from redundant words.

The grammatical means of securing brevity include:
(i) using the shortest words that will serve your purpose;
(ii) using a noun as an adjective, instead of a phrase or clause: as hotel room, government publications, etc.
(iii) using adjectives instead of phrases:

"An experiment carefully carried out would show ..." might be written "A careful experiment would show ..."
(iv) avoiding circumlocutions such as "in the majority of instances" (most), "to a considerable extent," etc.
(v) avoiding the use of two nouns that mean the same thing, as "intents and purposes," "satisfaction and happiness," etc.

You should be sparing in your use of adjectives. One adjective which expresses your meaning is better than two. A common error is to attempt to strengthen an adjective by putting an adverb before it, as "excessively," "immensely," "vastly," etc. Such exaggeration is usually ineffective.

(9) Although brevity is desirable, you must not pack so much information into a sentence that the reader cannot take it in. The rate at which information is presented can be excessive. Writing can be too concise: "The pulverized fuel is gravity-fed to a point where it meets the forced draught through a twelve-armed spider rotating rapidly to break up any lumps of coal that may have formed due to the coal particles adhering together." Kapp, who quotes this sentence in his book, *The Presentation of Technical Information,* remarks that it would not help the author of this sentence to tell him that he must be concise; and that he should be taught to force some extra words and a few full stops into his sentences.

Connecting Sentences Together

Sentences have to be linked together intelligibly if the reader is to follow the sequence of thought. This linking is more a matter of presenting your thoughts in the right order than a matter of grammar, but it will help you to make easy transitions from one thought to the next if you study the various conjunctions and linking phrases which are usually treated under the heading of "grammar."

The grammatical means of transition include:

(1) Conjunctions such as "and," "but," "although," "for."
(2) Adverbs and adverbial phrases such as "however," "moreover," "for example," "since this is so," "as we shall see," "nevertheless," "yet," "therefore," etc.
(3) Pronouns and articles—when you begin a sentence with "he" or "the" it refers back to a person or thing already defined.
(4) Repetitions of parts of the previous sentence.

Conjunctions such as "and" and "but" come first in the sentence. (Incidentally there is no rule against beginning sentences with "and" or "but.") The adverbs can be placed almost anywhere in the sentence, even at the end. It is said that "however" should not come at the beginning or at the end of the sentence. Even this rule may be broken, however.

You should take care when you use "but," "therefore," or any other connective word that the sense of the sentences does require the connective to be used. Therefore, for example, means "consequently," "for that reason." "But," as a conjunction, always introduces a contrast or a reason to the contrary. It is never a synonym for "and." "And" adds something like what has gone before; "but" adds something different.

No definite rule can be laid down as to how closely sentences should be linked together. A rambling string of sentences is as irritating as a rambling incoherent speech. But linking can be overdone. For instance, in this passage:

"Speculators and property-sharks have taken over the houses. These houses used to be let at moderate rents. The rents have now been raised so high that many of the tenants cannot afford them. These tenants have lost their homes . . ." The sentences are too explicitly linked, each topic following the next too mechanically. In linking your sentences you can leave the reader to do some of the work.

Paragraphs mark larger transitions. Each paragraph normally begins with a topic sentence, which announces what it is going to contain. Since each paragraph should be a unit, you should be able to give the reader, at the outset, a summary idea of what to expect. You need not, however, try too hard to construct a topic sentence. In narrative, particularly, there may be a number of intertwined events contained in a paragraph, so that no single event can be regarded as the core of the paragraph.

Writers are sometimes advised to vary sentence length within the paragraph. A long sentence followed by a shorter sentence is often effective, where the shorter sentence summarizes the points which have been amplified in the long one. Certainly an unbroken sequence of long sentences is tiresome, and a sequence of short ones disrupts the flow of ideas. But usually the length of your sentences will be varied enough without conscious effort on your part.

The average number of syllables per sentence varies from about eight in comic strips to about sixty in some eighteenth-century prose. An average figure for modern prose is about twenty syllables per sentence (as in this sentence). Academic authors average about thirty syllables per sentence.

The Organization of Written Materials

In any sort of technical exposition or reasoned argument presentation must follow a logical sequence. Before you begin to write on any factual topic you need to make an outline of the subject-matter before you start.

Any large task needs to be broken into manageable units; and you need to think carefully about the order of presentation of these units and how they are to be linked together. This task is most arduous in the review type of essay or article, in which you have to piece together evidence from many different sources on a number of complicated issues. Subheadings and subdivisions should always be used in essays and articles of any length, not only because they assist the reader, but also because they impose a useful discipline on the writer himself, and keep him from wandering away from the point.

Your first task is, of course, to do the necessary research and reading, and to amass materials. It has already been suggested that it is best to use cards to record each separate piece of information as it comes to hand. You must then think, decide on your main themes, and begin to select among your materials and reduce them to order.

This preparation inevitably takes more time than the writing itself, but it is a mistake to start writing before you have a definite plan and before you have thought matters out. Some of the most effective writers never set pen to paper until they have clear in their heads the entire scheme of what they mean to say. Others find a detailed written outline too constricting, and prefer to elaborate their ideas in the process of writing. It is true that many new ideas tend to occur in the course of writing, so that writing which has not been too rigidly planned may appear more spontaneous than that which follows a preformed scheme. The danger is that the new ideas may be irrelevant, and may lead you away from your main theme. An outline of some sort is therefore desirable in the interests of form and unity.

Rewriting

It has to be said that many writers find it so hard to express themselves clearly and logically that they expect to have to rewrite their material several times. They arrive at their final draft by a series of approximations. First a rough draft is made, and this is then written over, rephrased, and reordered with scissors and paste, until something like the desired product begins to emerge.

This procedure is, however, both a confession of literary failure and a waste of time. If you have ordinary literary talents you should be able to learn to write clearly and acceptably without the necessity of constant rewriting. Of course much practice, and much attention in the early stages to the mechanics of writing and composition, are needed before you can develop a lucid style. But in time you should be able to reach the stage where you do not have to think too much of words as you write, and your first draft can also be the final one.

Questions to Ask on Rereading

You should, then, learn to write in such a way that extensive rewriting can be avoided. But this does not mean that you should not carefully reread and correct what you have written. You should set your completed writing aside for a few days, and then look at it again, asking yourself such questions as these:

(1) Have I kept to my main themes? Or have I inserted padding and irrelevancies?

(2) Is each paragraph a natural unit? Is the transition from one topic to the next too abrupt? Are some topics left hanging in the air, inconclusively?

(3) Are any of my sentences too lengthy and involved? Is their sense always clear? Have I used any pronouns whose antecedents are unclear?

(4) Could I give the exact meaning of each word I have used? Have I used, as far as possible, concrete familiar words, and avoided vague words and pat, meaningless phrases?

(5) Is the general effect of my writing what I had intended? Is it too dull and heavy? Are there any passages which I am particularly proud of? (If so, strike them out, or subject them to severe criticism.)

(6) Have I consulted the convenience of the reader? Could I have done more to make his task easy by giving examples and illustrations?

Punctuation

Punctuation shows which words are to be taken together as units, and which are mere continuations of preceding words. Full stops, commas, etc., are substitutes for the pauses and intonations of speech. They assist the eye in reading by holding together words in units corresponding to thoughts. A few hundred years ago punctuation was much fuller than it is now because books were then often read aloud.

(1) The full-stop marks the end of a sentence. The only advice that needs to be given is that you should use it plentifully.

(2) The comma is more difficult. The modern tendency is not to use it too liberally. If in doubt leave the comma out.

Commas should be used:

(*a*) to set off words, phrases and clauses which do not form an essential part of the sentence or which interrupt the sequence of thought, e.g.:

"The town, far from the smoke of industry, is healthy."

"To be frank, we don't like the new neighbors."

(*b*) to separate a series of words, phrases and clauses, e.g.

"He was brought up on Latin, Greek and ancient history."

"He said that the pay was poor, that the work was hard, and that promotion was impossible."

(*c*) to separate clauses joined by conjunctions such as "and," "but," "for," "or," from the main part of the sentence. The comma is only necessary, however, if the subordinate clause is long, or if the subject of the sentence is changed:

"The sun is shining, but I have to stay in."

"The sun is shining but it won't shine for long."

Sometimes a sentence with a comma omitted may be obscure or ludicrous, e.g.

"While the keepers were eating the elephant got out."

If the meaning of a sentence depends on a comma, it is better to reconstruct the sentence.

(3) Semicolons represent a longer pause than a comma, but less than a full stop. They are useful if a sentence is getting too long. Some modern authors seldom use them, but there is no reason to be afraid of doing so.

(4) The colon is now little used, except to precede an explanation, or set of instructions. A colon with a dash after it is used to introduce a quotation or example.

(5) The long dash (—) is thought to be slovenly and incorrect by some, but may be used when a part of a sentence

needs to be separated from the main body more strongly than by a comma.

Spelling Mistakes

It is important to avoid spelling mistakes. In the first place their odd appearance distracts the reader's attention; in the second place they tend to be regarded as evidence of illiteracy and lack of a proper education.

Some people are poor spellers because they were taught as children to read in whole words and phrases, and have never learned to analyze words into their constituents.

Certain words are notoriously difficult to spell. Some 100 words account for about a third of all misspellings. Usually the errors are confined to one or two letters in the word.

If you know that you tend to misspell certain words, keep a list of them. Then take each word in turn and try to project it mentally, in every detail, on to a flat surface in front of you. If you are unable to visualize clearly every part of the word, look it up. Practice also spelling the words out loud, and writing them down many times.

Common misspellings include:

	Misspelling
achieve, believe	acheive, beleive
receive, deceive	recieve, decieve

The rule is: i before e, except after c, but there are common exceptions such as weigh, science.
Note that the final e is dropped before adding a suffix beginning with a vowel.

	Misspelled
coming, using.	comeing, useing.

Longish words with double letters in the middle are frequently misspelled.

	Misspelled
accommodate	accomodate or acommodate
embarrassment	embarassment or embarrasment
occurrence	occurence

Many misspellings arise from writing words as they are sounded as:

	Misspelled
definite	definate
dependent (adj.)	dependant
privilege	priviledge
separate	seperate
medicine	medecine

Avoid confusing "principle" (noun) and "principal" (adjective); and, of course, "there" and "their," and "two," "to" and "too."

Handwriting

There is evidence that the handwriting of college students is worse than that of fourteen-year-olds at school. At college notes often have to be taken quickly, and there is some danger that handwriting will deteriorate under the pressure for speed. Research has already been quoted to show that poorly written examination answers tend to be marked down. On this ground alone it is worth trying to improve your handwriting. Samuel Butler claimed that he improved the clarity of his thought when he took pains to write clearly.

Most people's handwriting contains one or two specific defects, which are easy to locate and remedy. A common source of difficulty is forming a letter in such a way that it looks like another letter, e.g. writing r like an undotted i, or d like cl or k like h.

It is quite easy to locate the defects in your handwriting.

(1) Give a typical specimen of your handwriting, about 500 words long, to two other students. Ask them to read through the specimen quickly and to put a mark under any letters or combination of letters which are at all difficult to read.

(2) Get your readers to tell you exactly which features of your writing caused trouble at each marked place.

(3) Tabulate your errors on a chart like the one given below. Total up the errors, and determine your most frequent illegibilities.

Handwriting Chart

a like u	h like l	r like i
a „ o	i dot misplaced	r „ half u
b „ li	k like h	s indistinct (final s)
c „ e	l closed	s like r
d „ cl	l too short	t „ l
e closed	m like w	t cross omitted
e too high	n „ u	u like a
g „ y	n „ v	v „ i
h „ li	o „ a	w „ ri
h „ b	o closed	

Words crowded—too little space between words.

Words broken—breaks between syllables.

Words joined—failure to take pen off paper between words.

Loops too long—so that they reach down into the line below or up into the line above.

Writing too slanted.

Having tabulated your most frequent illegibilities, you will probably find that a few letters are causing most of the difficulties. Take particular care in forming these letters until you form the habit of writing them legibly.

Summary

Ways of improving your writing include enlarging your vocabulary by extensive reading, and learning the principles of grammar or syntax, which are now seldom formally taught in schools.

Short familiar words are generally to be preferred to lengthy circumlocutions, but in writing on technical matters the appropriate technical vocabulary has to be used. Avoid jargon and words whose meaning has been debased.

Some general rules are given for the construction of sentences and for connecting sentences together.

Before tackling any large piece of writing an outline plan is desirable. You should avoid the necessity of rewriting, but critically examine your efforts after laying your writing aside for a few days.

Some advice is given about punctuation and spelling, and a scheme for improving handwriting is suggested.

For further reading:

Kapp, R. O., *The Presentation of Technical Information*, Constable and Co., London, 1948.
Gowers, Sir Ernest, *Plain Words*, H.M.S.O., London, 1948.

CHAPTER ELEVEN

SIMPLE MATHEMATICS

THIS CHAPTER is not intended for mathematical specialists, but for those who have perhaps done little mathematics for some years, and wish to renew their knowledge of elementary mathematical operations.

The ability to do mathematics is often thought of as rather a special skill—there are many otherwise able people who have special difficulty with it. And it is true that mathematics comes much more easily to some than to others. Many people whose training has been mainly in the arts decide that they are no good at it, and some develop a dislike and even a fear of the subject quite early in their school careers.

But in all the natural and social sciences, competence in elementary mathematics is becoming increasingly important. This chapter therefore sets out the elementary rules and principles of arithmetic and algebraic operations. Ignorance of these rules probably accounts for more of the difficulties in mathematics than any other cause.

Symbols

$+$, $-$, $\div$ and $\times$ refer to addition, subtraction, division and multiplication. Parentheses and brackets are also used to indicate multiplication, e.g. (6) (7) means 6×7.

If no multiplication sign is needed, the product of a and b is written ab.

Division is usually indicated not by $\div$ but by a bar:

a divided by b is written a/b or $\dfrac{a}{b}.$

Other symbols are:

$=$ is equal to.
$\equiv$ is identically equal to.
$\doteqdot$ is approximately equal to.
$<$ is less than.
$>$ is greater than.
$\leqq$ is less than or equal to.

186

$\geqq$ is greater than or equal to.

$\neq$ is not equal to.

$\pm$ plus or minus.

$a \sim b$ means the difference between a and b.

The omission of terms in a sequence is shown by dots:

$1, 2, 3, 4 \ldots 100$ means all integers from 1 to 100, and $X_1 + X_2 + X_3 \ldots X_{10}$ means the sum of all the 10 terms from X_1 to X_{10}.

A vertical line is used to mean 'when' or 'if':

$x = 5 \mid y = 6$ means x is 5 when y is 6.

A small figure written above and to the right of a symbol is called an index or exponent:

$2^3 = 2 \times 2 \times 2$.

$a^2 b^3 = aabbb$.

Small figures and letters used as subscripts have no numerical significance, e.g. $n_1 + n_2$ merely serves to distinguish one number or group or sample, n_1, from another, n_2.

The Order of Operations

The rules about the order in which arithmetic operations, (addition, subtraction, multiplication and division) are performed are as follows:

(1) The order in which numbers are added or multiplied does not affect the result.

$2 + 3 + 4 = 4 + 3 + 2 = 9$. $2 \times 3 \times 4 = 4 \times 3 \times 2 = 24$.

$a + b + c = c + b + a$ $abc = cba$.

(2) When both multiplication and addition (or subtraction) are involved, the multiplication should be performed first unless brackets indicate otherwise:

$130 - 20 \times 5 = 30$ but $(130 - 20) \times 5 = 550$.

(3) When both division and addition (or subtraction) are involved, the division should be performed first, unless brackets indicate otherwise:

$130 + 20 \div 10 = 132$ but $(130 + 20) \div 10 = 15$.

(4) When both multiplication and division are involved, brackets must be used to indicate the order of operations:

$$12 \div (2 \times 3) = 2.$$

(5) Brackets and parentheses are used to show that the terms enclosed within them should be treated as a single number:

$5(12 - 2) = 5(10) = 50$ or $5(12 - 2) = 60 - 10 = 50$ and $x(a + b + c) = xa + xb + xc$.

Note that the multiplication is distributed over all terms in the brackets.

(6) The expression under a radical sign is likewise treated as a single number:

$$\sqrt{20 - 3} = \sqrt{17}.$$

That is, the operations underneath the radical are carried out before the root is taken:

$$\sqrt{16 + 9} = \sqrt{25} = 5$$
$$But \ \sqrt{16} + \sqrt{9} = 4 + 3 = 7.$$

(7) In fractions, the numerator is treated as a single number, and the denominator as a single number:

$$\frac{4 + 6}{5 + 5} = \frac{10}{10} \ or \ (4 + 6)/(5 + 5) = 10/10$$
$$\frac{18 - 3}{5} = \frac{18}{5} - \frac{3}{5} = \frac{15}{5}.$$

Operations with Zero and One

The product of zero and any other number is zero:

(9) (0) = 0.

Regardless of the size of the divisor $0/a = 0$.

Division by zero is not permissible.

The product of a number, a, by 1 is a: $(a)(1) = a$.

The quotient of a number, a, divided by 1 is a: $a/1 = a$.

The quotient of a number, a, divided by itself is 1, $\frac{a}{a} = 1$, except when $a = 0$. From this it follows that 1 can be transformed into any fraction having the same numerator and denominator:

$$1 = \frac{a}{a} \ or \ \frac{a^2 + 2ab - b^2}{a^2 + 2ab - b^2}.$$

Positive and Negative Numbers

Numbers can be both positive and negative. On any scale, the numbers above any reference point may be treated as positive and those below as negative. Examples are degrees above and below freezing-point on a thermometer or scores above and below a mean score.

(1) If all numbers have the same sign, they are simply added and the sum given the common sign:

$$(-2) + (-4) + (-6) = -12$$

(2) When two numbers to be added have unlike signs, the sum is the difference between the two numbers and the sign of the sum is the sign of the large number:

$$4 + (-8) = -4$$

(3) To add several numbers with unlike signs, the positive and negative numbers are added separately. The difference be-

tween the two sums is then taken and the sign of the larger sum is attached:

$$2 - 4 + 5 - 13 = -10$$

(4) In subtracting positive and negative numbers the sign of the subtrahend (number to be subtracted) is changed and addition is performed as above:

$$4 - (-6) = 10$$
$$-4 - (-8) = 4$$
$$-4 - (+8) = -12$$

(5) In multiplication, numbers with like signs yield positive products; numbers with unlike signs yield negative products:

$$4 \times -4 = -16$$
$$-4 \times -4 = 16$$

(6) The division of numbers with like signs yields positive quotients; the division of numbers with unlike signs negative quotients:

$$-12 \div -4 = 3$$
$$12 \div -4 = -3$$

Fractions

(1) Multiplying or dividing both the numerator and denominator by the same number (other than zero) does not change the value of a fraction.

Complicated fractions can thus be reduced to more simple ones:

$$\frac{800}{900} = \frac{8}{9} \qquad \frac{.01}{.04} = \frac{1}{4} \qquad \frac{2a^2}{4ax} = \frac{a}{2x}$$

(2) But adding or subtracting the same number in both numerator and denominator does, usually, change the value of the fraction.

In adding and subtracting fractions you must obtain a common denominator and then add the numerators:

$$\frac{1}{3} + \frac{4}{5} = \frac{5}{15} + \frac{12}{15} = \frac{17}{15} = 1\frac{2}{15}$$

In general:

$$\frac{a}{b} + \frac{c}{d} = \frac{ad}{bd} + \frac{bc}{bd} = \frac{ad + bc}{bd}$$

(3) To multiply fractions you simply multiply the numerators and multiply the denominators:

$$\frac{6}{7} \times \frac{2}{5} = \frac{12}{35}$$

In general:

$$\frac{a}{b} \times \frac{c}{d} = \frac{ac}{bd}$$

(4) To divide fractions you invert the divisor and multiply:

$$\frac{1/3}{2/5} = \frac{1}{3} \times \frac{5}{2} = \frac{5}{6}$$

In general:

$$\frac{a}{b} \div \frac{c}{d} = \frac{a}{b} \times \frac{d}{c}$$

(5) If 1 is divided by any number n, this fraction is the reciprocal of n. Thus 1/5 is the reciprocal of 5.

Division by a number is equivalent to multiplication by the reciprocal of the number:

$$\frac{7}{20} = 7 \times \frac{1}{20} = (7)\,(.05) = .35$$

$$\frac{a}{n} = a \times \frac{1}{n}$$

In using calculating machines, it is often quicker to multiply by the reciprocal than to divide.

Decimals

In adding and subtracting decimals make sure that you keep the decimal points in line, and that the decimal point in the answer lies directly under the decimal points of the figures added or subtracted:

$$
\begin{array}{r}
2.38 \\
+1.001 \\
\hline
3.381
\end{array}
\qquad
\begin{array}{r}
7.084 \\
-1.13 \\
\hline
5.954
\end{array}
$$

In multiplying decimals, multiply as with whole numbers. Then begin at the right-hand end of the product, and point off as many decimal places as there are in the multiplier and multiplicand together:

$$
\begin{array}{r}
.03 \\
\times .09 \\
\hline
.0027
\end{array}
$$
Both multiplier and multiplicand have 2 decimal places so their product must have 4.

$$
\begin{array}{r}
120 \\
\times .02 \\
\hline
2.40
\end{array}
$$
Here the multiplicand has no decimal places. The multiplier has 2. Their product therefore has $(0 + 2) = 2$ decimal places.

Before you start dividing one decimal by another you should

drop any zeros to the right of the decimal, e.g. for .25000 write .25.

Then make the divisor into a whole number by moving the decimal point to the right the appropriate number of places. As you must treat both the numerator and denominator of a fraction in the same way, you must now move the decimal point of the dividend by the same number of places. Then perform ordinary long division:

$$\frac{0.03}{.25} = \frac{3}{25} = .12.$$

Other examples:

$$\frac{.42}{.002} = \frac{420}{2} = 210.$$

$$\frac{.007}{.09} = \frac{0.7}{9} \left(\text{or} \frac{7}{90} \right) = .0778.$$

Proportions and Percentages

If you wish to find what proportion of a sum or total number a given number is, divide the number by the sum or total, e.g. if 75 out of 600 urban households keep a dog, and you wish to know what proportion of the total 600 keep a dog, divide 75 by 600 to obtain the answer, .125.

To express a proportion as a percentage multiply the proportion by 100. In the above example, for instance, the percentage of households keeping dogs is:

$$.125 \times 100 = 12.5 \text{ per cent.}$$

Conversely to translate a percentage into a proportion, divide the percentage by 100.

Reversing these operations, if you are given a proportion or percentage, and wish to convert it to the actual number which the proportion or percentage represents, multiply the proportion by the total number:

$$.125 \times 600 = 75$$

or multiply the percentage by the total number and divide by 100:

$$\frac{12.5 \times 600}{100} = 75.$$

Note that it is misleading to give figures in percentages when the sum total of observations is less than 100.

Speed and Accuracy in Computation

In work such as adding long columns of digits it is as well to work as rapidly as possible. In this kind of operation speed and accuracy go together. If you work slowly your attention will fluctuate and errors will arise. In a group of students the fastest will usually be able to add at four or five times the rate of the slowest, and more accurately.

Facility in computation is mostly the result of practice. If you wish to become skilled in mental arithmetic, you must practice doing sums in your head. Get into the habit of making estimates of such problems as the number of times a car wheel revolves each minute when the car is travelling at 60 m.p.h., etc.

Before performing any calculation, the best safeguard against gross error is to estimate the answer in advance. If you divide 314 by 26, for example, it should be obvious that the answer will be approximately $300/25 = 12$. In dividing decimals it helps to move the decimal points the same number of places in divisor and dividend, so as to approximate familiar, manageable numbers:

$$.56 \div .069 \simeq 56/7 \simeq 8$$
$$3.972 \div 1.93 \simeq 4/2 \simeq 2$$

In estimating the answers to multiplications it sometimes helps to move the decimal point in the two numbers to be multiplied the same number of places in opposite directions:

$$.051 \times 2400 = 5.1 \times 24 \simeq 5 \times 25 \simeq 125$$
$$18.39 \times 297.6 \simeq 2 \times 3,000 \simeq 6,000$$

A slide rule is one of the best checks against gross blunders in arithmetic. Learning to use a slide rule is in fact one of the best disciplines in computation, because the slide rule forces you to make rough assessments of the answer, and of the position of the decimal point. Even if you use it for no other purpose, you should learn to use a slide rule for multiplication and division.

In finding the average of a set of fairly similar numbers, arithmetic can be saved by coding the scores. If you have 10 scores—206, 217, 224, 227, 228, 231, 236, 241, 245, 258, you can obviously subtract 200 from each score, the mean being $200 + 313/10 = 231.3$. Thus in calculating a mean it is always possible to subtract a constant from the scores, in order to save arithmetic. This amounts to taking an arbitrary figure for the mean and working in deviations from this arbitrary mean. When the arbitrary mean is M^1, the deviations from it x^1, and n the number of scores the mean $\overline{X} = M^1 + \dfrac{\Sigma x^1}{n}$.

(Σ = the sum of) In the above example $\overline{X} = 200 + \dfrac{313}{10}$.

Such coding of scores is commonly used in statistics where large numbers of scores are involved.

Indices

a^n means 'a to the nth power' or 'a to the nth'.

The number n is the *index* or *exponent* and the number a is the *base*. Thus a^2 is a squared or a raised to the power of 2, or $a \times a$. a^4 is a raised to the fourth power or $a \times a \times a \times a$. Indices need not be whole numbers. $a^{3.5}$ would lie somewhere between a^3 and a^4.

Indices can have fractional values. These are then roots.

$a^{\frac{1}{2}} = \sqrt{a}$ and $a^{\frac{1}{4}} = \sqrt[4]{a}$

Indices can be negative, as a^{-2} or a^{-4}

These are equivalent to $\dfrac{1}{a^2}$ and $\dfrac{1}{a^4}$

Thus:

$$a^{-n} = \frac{1}{a^n} \quad \text{e.g. } 3^{-2} = \frac{1}{3^2}$$

$$a^{\frac{1}{n}} = \sqrt[n]{a} \quad\quad 3^{\frac{1}{2}} = \sqrt{3}$$

$$a^{-\frac{1}{n}} = \frac{1}{\sqrt[n]{a}} \quad\quad 3^{-\frac{1}{2}} = \frac{1}{\sqrt{3}}$$

Operations with Indices

Addition $(a^m)(a^n) = a^{m+n}$
  e.g. $(2^2)(2^3) = 2^5$
    $(2^{-2})(2^5) = 2^3$

Subtraction $\dfrac{a^m}{a^n} = a^{(m-n)}$

  e.g. $\dfrac{2^5}{2^3} = 2^2$

    $\dfrac{2^3}{2^{-2}} = 2^5$

Multiplication $a^{(m)n} = a^{mn}$
  e.g. $(2^3)^2 = 2^6$
    $(2^{-2})^2 = 2^{-4}$

Division $\sqrt[n]{a^m}$ $= a^{\frac{m}{n}}$

e.g. $\sqrt{2^4}$ $= 2^{\frac{4}{2}} = 2^2$

            $\sqrt[3]{2^7}$ $= 2^{\frac{7}{3}}$

Note also that:

(i) $(ab)^n$ $= (a^n)\,(b^n)$

e.g. $(2 \times 5)^2 = 2^2 \times 5^2$

(ii) $\left(\dfrac{a}{b}\right)^n$ $= \dfrac{a^n}{b^n}$

e.g. $\left(\dfrac{2}{5}\right)^2$ $= \dfrac{2^2}{5^2}$

(iii) a^0 $= 1$

$\therefore$ a^0 $= a^{n-n} = \dfrac{a^n}{a^n} = 1$

Logarithms

Logarithms can be used for multiplication, division, and for extracting roots, and raising to a power.

Common logarithms use the base 10. A logarithm of a number to the base 10 is the exponent of 10 which equals the number. Some simple examples of numbers and their logarithms are:

Number	Exponent of 10	Logarithms
1000	10^3	3.0000
100	10^2	2.0000
10	10^1	1.0000
1	10^0	0.0000
.1	10^{-1}	$\bar{1}.0000$
.01	10^{-2}	$\bar{2}.0000$
.001	10^{-3}	$\bar{3}.0000$

Most numbers, of course, are not simple multiples of ten. The logarithm of 5 for example is 0.6990, to four decimal places. Four-figure tables of logarithms do for most practical purposes.

The logarithm of any positive number has two parts: an integer called the characteristic, and a decimal fraction called the mantissa. The characteristic determines the position of the decimal point. The mantissa determines the sequence of digits. The log. of 1,000 = 3.000; 3 is the characteristic, and .0000 the mantissa.

Thus you determine the characteristic by inspection of the decimal point and get the mantissa from a table of logarithms.

The rule for the characteristic is: when the number is larger than 1 its characteristic is one less than the number of digits to the left of the decimal point. When the number is smaller than 1, its characteristic is negative and one more than the number of zeros between the decimal point and the first non-zero digit.

Get a table of logs, and check that the logarithm of 50 is 1.6990, of 5 0.6990, of 0.5 $\bar{1}$.6990, of .05 $\bar{2}$.6990.

Note that the mantissa is always positive in sign. The characteristic can be either positive or negative. When the characteristic is negative and the mantissa is positive, they must be treated as two separate numbers. This is important in finding the square root of a decimal fraction. (See second example below.)

The rules for computation with logarithms can be described in a few simple rules:

Computation with numbers	Computation with logarithms
$A \times B$	$\log A + \log B$
$A \div B$	$\log A - \log B$
A^n	$n \log A$
$\sqrt[n]{A}$	$\dfrac{1}{n} \log A$

Example: $7.307 \times 0.9742 \times 0.478$

$$\log 7.307 \quad = 0.8637$$
$$\log\ \ .09742 = \bar{2}.9886$$
$$\log 0.478 \quad = \bar{1}.6794$$

$$\log \text{product} = \bar{1}.5317$$
$$\text{Product} \quad = 0.3402$$

Example: Find $\sqrt{0.6742}$

$$\log 0.6742 \quad = \bar{1}.8288$$

To find the square root the logarithm has to be divided by 2. This is awkward as the logarithm stands. Since the characteristic and the mantissa are separate numbers, one negative and the other positive, you must arrange matters so that the characteristic is divisible by the divisor. Remembering that

$$\bar{1}.8288 = -1 + .8288$$

if -1 is added to the characteristic and $+1$ is added to the mantissa, the value will still be the same.

$$\overline{1}.8288 = \overline{2} + 1.8288$$
$$\text{then dividing by } 2, \overline{1}.9144$$
$$= 0.8211$$

Example: Find $\sqrt[5]{4.785} \times \sqrt[3]{.347}$

⅕ log 4.785 = ⅕ of 0.6799   = 0.1360

⅓ log .347 = ⅓ (−3 + 2.5403) = $\overline{1}.8468$

Sum $\overline{1}.9828$ = .9612

Square Roots

The most practical ways of finding square roots are by logarithms or by a table of squares and square roots. The method using logarithms is described under that head.

If you have to do much statistical work you should have a *Table of Squares, Cubes, Square Roots, Cube Roots and Reciprocals.*

Many textbooks carry tables of squares from 1 to 1,000. To find the square root of a number you should first point off the number in pairs, on either side of the decimal point. Thus

4023.07 becomes 40 23 . 07

When the number of figures to the left or to the right of the decimal point is odd, add a zero:

292.4 becomes 02 92 . 40

The square root will have one figure for every pair in the number, as pointed off. For example:

$$\sqrt{02\ 92\ .\ 40} = 17.1$$

(since there are two pairs to the left and one pair to the right of the decimal point).

Note that the square root of any number less than 1 is always greater than the number itself:

e.g. $\sqrt{.49} = .7$

To multiply two roots or radicals, multiply their radicands (i.e. the number enclosed by the root sign):

$$\sqrt{a}\ \sqrt{b} = \sqrt{ab}$$

To divide one radical by another radical divide the radicand of the first by the radicand of the second:

$$\sqrt{a}/\sqrt{b} = \sqrt{a/b}$$

A radicand can be factorized into two numbers, as an aid to computation:

e.g. $\sqrt{810} = \sqrt{81}\ \sqrt{10} = 9\sqrt{10}$

$\sqrt{8} = \sqrt{4}\ \sqrt{2} = 2\sqrt{2}$

$\sqrt{75} = \sqrt{25}\ \sqrt{3} = 5\sqrt{3}$

Equations

You should be able to rearrange the form of a simple equation, or to change the subject of a formula.

The simple rule is that whatever is done to one side of an equation must also be done to the other side:

(i) The same number can be added to each side.

(ii) The same number can be subtracted from each side.

(These two rules mean that, when a term is removed from one side of an equation, it appears on the other side with its sign changed.)

(iii) Each side can be multiplied by the same number.

(iv) Each side can be divided by the same number.

Also, in general, the root may be taken of each side, or each side may be raised to the same power.

The rules for solving a simple equation are:

(1) Clear the equation of fractions by multiplying both sides by the least common denominator.

(2) Get all the terms containing the unknown on one side, and all the other terms on the other.

(3) Combine the terms containing the unknown.

(4) Divide both sides by the coefficient of the unknown.

Example 1. Solve $\dfrac{2a}{3} - \dfrac{x}{2} + a = 4.$ for x

(multiply both sides by 6)

$4a - 3x + 6a = 24$

$-3x + 10a = 24$

$-3x = 24 - 10a$ (10a subtracted from both sides)

$x = \dfrac{10a - 24}{3}$ (Divide both sides by -3)

Example 2. Solve $\dfrac{15}{2} = 4 - \dfrac{a + 5}{1 - a}$ for a

$15(1 - a) = 8(1 - a) - 2(a + 5)$ (multiply both sides by $2(1 - a)$)

$$15 - 15a = 8 - 8a - 2a - 10$$
$$15 - 15a = -10a - 2$$
$$-5a = -17$$
$$a = \frac{17}{5}$$

Example 3. Solve

$$a = b \sqrt{\frac{x}{c-d}} \quad \text{for } d$$

$$a^2 = \frac{b^2 x}{c-d} \quad \text{(squaring both sides)}$$

$$a^2(c-d) = b^2 x \quad \text{(multiply both sides by } (c-d)\text{)}$$

$$(c-d) = \frac{b^2 x}{a^2} \quad \text{(both sides divided by } a^2\text{)}$$

$$-d = \frac{b^2 x}{a^2} - c \quad \text{(} c \text{ subtracted from both sides)}$$

$$d = c - \frac{b^2 x}{a^2} \quad \text{(both sides multiplied by } -1\text{)}$$

Graphs

Graphs are used to indicate the relationship between two variables. The horizontal scale of a graph is called the abscissa and the vertical scale the ordinate. By convention independent variables are designated 'x' variables, and laid out along the abscissa; dependent variables are designated 'y' variables and laid out along the ordinate. In a plot of the amount remembered after various time intervals, for example, the amount remembered is *dependent* on the time which has passed since the original learning. The amount remembered is therefore the dependent variable, set out along the ordinate; the time since learning is the independent variable, set out along the abscissa. As another example, we might have gain in weight in pounds on the ordinate as the dependent variable, plotted against amount of food consumed on the abscissa. (See Fig. 23 overleaf.) To read this graph you locate a value for food consumed on the abscissa, then erect an imaginary line from that point upward until it meets the line; and then run an imaginary line horizontally to the ordinate to find the gain in weight.

In this case the line is straight: gain in weight is approximately a linear function of food consumed. The line in fact represents an equation:

$$y = .26x - 22$$

In Fig. 24 a number of linear equations are plotted:
Line A represents the equation $y = .5x$

Line B $y = .5x + 8$

Line B $y = .5x + 8$ has a slope of .5 and intersects the y axis at $y = 8$. The general formula for a straight line is

$$y = a + bx$$

where b is the slope of the line and a is the y intercept.

Such functions are useful because they enable many additional values to be predicted from the observation of a few.

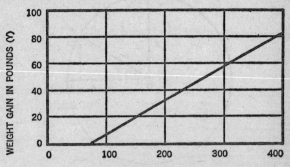

Fig. 23. *Relationship of amount of feed eaten by pigs to gain in weight*

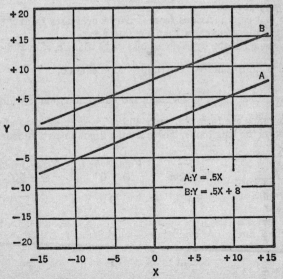

Fig. 24. *Examples of linear functions*

Trigonometry

In a circle with radius length r the line OP may be imagined as free to rotate from the horizontal position to the vertical. Let the angle which the line makes with the horizontal be called Θ.

In the horizontal position $\Theta = 0°$, in the vertical position $\Theta = 90°$.

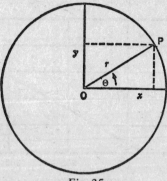

Fig. 25

OP has coordinates x and y, its projections on the horizontal and vertical axes.

Note that as Θ increases from $0-90°$ x decreases from $x = r$ to $x = 0$ and y increases from $y = 0$ to $y = r$.

And, since r is the hypotenuse of a right triangle, $r^2 = x^2 + y^2$.

As Θ approaches $90°$ the ratio $\dfrac{x}{r}$ approaches 0,

$\dfrac{y}{r}$ approaches 1, $\dfrac{x}{y}$ approaches 0, and $\dfrac{y}{x}$ becomes infinitely large.

Six ratios are formed by x, y and r. These ratios depend on Θ, not on the length of r. These are the trigonometric functions of Θ.

Ratio	Function	Value when $\Theta = 0°$	Value when $\Theta = 90°$
$\dfrac{y}{r}$	Sine	0	1
$\dfrac{y}{x}$	Tangent	0	∞
$\dfrac{r}{x}$	Secant	1	∞

The angle $90 - \odot$ is called the complement of $\odot$.

Thus the cosine of $\odot$ is the complement's sine, or sine of $(90 - \odot)$.

Its functions can be obtained from the functions of $\odot$ by interchanging x and y in the above ratios.

		Value when $\odot = 0°$	*Value when* $\odot = 90°$
$\dfrac{x}{r}$	cosine	1	0
$\dfrac{x}{y}$	cotangent	∞	0
$\dfrac{r}{y}$	cosecant	∞	1

For further reading:

Walker, Helen M., *Mathematics Essential for Elementary Statistics*, Holt, New York, 1951

CHAPTER TWELVE

THE PHYSICAL ENVIRONMENT

Far from the higher animals being indifferent to
their surroundings, they are on the contrary in
close and intimate relation to them, so that their
equilibrium is the result of compensation established as continually and as exactly as if by a very
sensitive balance.

CLAUDE BERNARD

WE now turn to the physical conditions of work, such as
lighting, heating and ventilation. You may think that these
things are relatively unimportant, or that they may usually
be taken for granted, and, to some extent, this is true. Lighting, heating and ventilation and their effect on work output
used to be the stock-in-trade of industrial psychologists. More
recently it has become the fashion to decry their importance
and lay more emphasis on motivation and attitudes to work.
Clearly your motivation is of more importance than the
physical conditions of your study room. Yet motivation is
complex and difficult to manipulate, whereas it is quite simple
to ensure that you have adequate lighting, for example, in
your study. Very often your evening work output will be influenced by such factors as the level of illumination in the
room, the distance you are sitting from the fire, and the kind
of chair you are sitting in. Even if these factors only affect
your working efficiency to the extent of 5–10 per cent, it is
worth paying attention to them, since faults can fairly easily
be set right.

Lighting

The general level of illumination in your study room should
be adequate, the light should be well distributed, and there

should not be glare or sharp contrasts of light and shade. These requirements sound simple enough, but freedom from glare is not always easy to attain.

The general level of illumination is measured in foot-candles, or in lumens per square foot (the two units are identical). A 100-watt lamp gives about 10 foot-candles at a distance of 52 inches and 25 foot-candles at 34 inches. In general, fine work demands a high level of illumination. You need more light to read small print or Greek or algebra comfortably than you need for ordinary 10-point type. Performance, such as reading speed, typically increases up to a certain critical level of illumination, after which there is little improvement even if the light is greatly increased. This critical level is between 4 and 6 foot-candles for ordinary reading, and about 20 foot-candles for threading a needle or making lace. It is easy enough to obtain these levels with ordinary 100- or 150-watt electric lamps.

Even distribution of light and avoidance of glare are much more difficult to ensure. There are four main types of shades and light-fittings: (1) direct, (2) semi-direct, (3) indirect, and (4) semi-indirect.

The direct type is the worst, and probably the most common, such as a low-hanging ceiling fixture which exposes the eye to direct glare from the lamp. Consider the glare that arises from the headlights of oncoming cars when driving at night. The glare tends to obscure whatever else might be seen in other portions of the visual field. The bright oncoming headlights cover the rest of the retina with stray illumination. In the same way, in lesser degree, your vision will suffer if unshaded light is present in the periphery or your field of vision.

An example of the semi-direct is the white glass globe, enclosing the lamp, which diffuses the light, much of it being reflected from the ceiling. This type is often used in offices. In indirect lighting all the light goes to the ceiling and upper walls, whence it is diffused about the room. A hanging fitting with an opaque circular reflector below the lamp is an example. In the semi-indirect type the reflector is translucent and allows some of the light to reach the working surface direct. You can see from the table that indirect lighting is very much to be preferred to the other types of lighting.

Table: Loss in visual efficiency during reading under four types of illumination.

Type of illumination	Percentage loss after 2 hours	Percentage loss after 3 hours
Daylight	5	6
Indirect	10	9
Semi-indirect	34	72
Direct	37	81

(Visual efficiency was taken as the ratio of clear to blurred vision.)

Uniform distribution and avoidance of glare are best attained by indirect lighting. It is not usually practicable, however, to obtain adequate local illumination by this means. Hence some combination of local and general illumination is required. Local lighting alone, as by a desk lamp, causes too much contrast of light and shade in the room. The retina of the eye adapts to the general level of illumination. Moreover, if you have a bright light in the periphery of your visual field there is a reflex tendency to keep looking at it, resulting in visual fatigue. The background lighting and the local lighting should not be too dissimilar, a ratio of about 1 : 3 being desirable.

For practical purposes this means that you should have an indirect or semi-indirect light for general illumination, and a standard lamp or desk lamp directly over your work. The desk lamp should not have an opaque shade, as this produces a bright area of light surrounded by shadows. (Most commercially available study lamps are of this undesirable type.) An ordinary table lamp with a semi-transparent shade is better, but the bottom of the shade should be about 20 inches above the table top so that the lampshade itself is outside the field of vision.

As a temporary expedient to shield the eyes from glare, you can wear an eyeshade of the type worn by tennis players.

Nowadays tubular fluorescent lighting is being increasingly used, as it provides a high level of illumination at low cost. This form of lighting can be fatiguing, however. There is 50-cycle flicker at the ends of the tubes, which therefore need to be shaded. This is not always done in the cheaper forms of shades, and sometimes causes odd stroboscopic effects on rotating machinery in workshops.

Ventilation and Heating

From the point of view of general efficiency, the main requirements are (1) pure air to breathe and (2) suitable air temperature and air movement, so that body temperature can be maintained without discomfort.

In breathing, oxygen is taken into the system and carbon dioxide is excreted. The percentage composition of fresh inspired air and expired air is given in the table:

	Inspired Air	Expired Air
Oxygen	20.96	16.4
Nitrogen	79	79.5
Carbon dioxide	0.04	4.1

Thus air that is breathed once loses about 4 per cent of its oxygen and gains about 4 per cent carbon dioxide.

If a man shuts himself up in a room with no means of ventilation, the air gradually loses its oxygen and gains a corresponding volume of carbon dioxide. After a time he feels all the usual effects of poor ventilation, such as headache and nausea. Allowing him to breathe fresh air from outside does not relieve these symptoms, however, and another man outside the chamber can breathe the foul air from inside without much ill effect. Hence the main reason for fresh air is that it is cooler and ventilates the body surfaces, not that it supplies much more oxygen than stale air.

The oxygen content of air is usually ample, staying remarkably constant at 20.9 per cent in both city and country. In city fogs the oxygen percentage may fall slightly, and there are injurious elements, such as sulphur, in the air in industrial areas. But the stalest of air in enclosed rooms still usually has an ample content of oxygen; the physiologists tell us that the oxygen percentage has to fall to about 14 per cent before signs of anoxia such as rapid breathing and blueness of the skin become evident. Excess carbon dioxide in the air is more likely to cause discomfort, as its effects are to displace oxygen in the blood, producing a kind of anoxia. About 5 per cent of carbon dioxide produces discomfort and headache, but even under the most overcrowded conditions the carbon dioxide percentage is unlikely to rise above about 0.5 per cent. In submarines a limited quantity of air is often breathed and rebreathed, until after a few hours a light will not burn in it. Submarines, however, carry devices for removing carbon dioxide from the air.

The temperature and moisture content of the air, then, usually have a more marked physiological effect than its chemical composition. But the chemical purity of the air is important, if only because stale stagnant air is much more likely to lead to respiratory infections than fresh circulating air. Expired air contains various organic matters, which although present in minute quantities, may have a harmful effect on the system. Lack of ventilation in a crowded room also results in many offensive odors. For these reasons good room ventilation, without drafts, is desirable, partly to prevent the accumulation of organic impurities and partly to avoid any lack of oxygen and concentration of carbon dioxide.

Air should not contain more than about 0.05 per cent of carbon dioxide. This means that each person needs a room of about 1,000 cubic feet into which about 2,000 cubic feet of fresh air are admitted each hour. The traditional advice to sleep with the window open is still good advice, at least for those in good health. In the waking hours, close and stuffy atmospheres may produce slight anoxia, and thus prevent the brain from working at maximum efficiency.

Temperature

Body temperature is affected not only by air temperature, but by the moisture content and rate of movement of the air, and by radiation from the body to surrounding objects. Roughly speaking, a temperature of 60–70°F. is considered best for mental work. Temperature in fact makes little difference to mental performance, at any rate over short periods, illustrating once again the adaptability of the human organism, but working under conditions of extreme heat or cold certainly involves more effort and more discomfort. Those who are accustomed to outdoor work and exercise are much less sensitive to heat and cold indoors than others.

Where to Study

Quiet and freedom from distraction are essential for private study. There is everything to be said for habitually studying in the same place. Books and materials are at hand, and do not have to be transported from one place to another. The familiar room provides the right atmosphere and stimulus for work.

Unfortunately it is not always easy to find this desirable environment. If you have to live in lodgings, you may have to live with non-students who do not realize that quiet and privacy are necessary for study; and even if your privacy is respected, you may still be distracted by noise or music or by the mere awareness that others are "enjoying themselves," while you are working. Often friends and associates are the worst enemies of study, if they keep dropping in on you for gossip or idle conversation, or try and tempt you away for a drink, a game of cards, etc. The only remedy against frittering your time away in this fashion is to be adamant in keeping set hours for work, and in letting your friends know what these hours are. All productive workers are forced to set aside certain hours for work, and to insist that they must not be disturbed during these hours by telephone calls, visitors, etc.

A study, then, is usually the best place for serious work. There are some students, however, who have a perfectly suitable study room, but still find it hard to work there. There may be a radio to turn on, a photograph of a sweetheart to gaze upon, food and drink temptingly available, etc. Also it is easy to fall into a daydream. Dr. Johnson wrote:

"Severe and connected attention is preserved but for a short time, and when a man shuts himself up in his closet, and bends his thoughts to the discussion of any abstruse question, he will find his faculties continually stealing away to more pleasing entertainment."

Only those who are strongly motivated are able to work for long in solitude. Others may find it easier to work in libraries. Research in fact shows that students who habitually work in libraries do better than those who do not. The sight of others working sometimes makes it easier to get down to work; behavior is more disciplined; there are rules against talking, etc. So if you are a person who is strongly affected by external stimulation you may find it easier to work in a library or classroom, where others are also working.

Study Furniture

Tension of the musculature facilitates mental activity. You can do better work sitting upright on a hard chair than slumped in an easy chair or lying on a bed.

If you watch someone who is doing hard mental work you will notice that his whole body is slightly tensed. Experiments have shown that a moderate degree of constant pressure on a hand dynamometer, for example, facilitates learning. Learning was also facilitated while maintaining a 14 lb. weight against a pulley. Conversely, muscular relaxation leads to mental lassitude.

It follows that study is best done while sitting at a desk or table and maintaining an erect posture. Since you will sit for many hours at your desk or table, you should pay attention to their height and dimensions. The desk should be of a certain size, at least 4 feet by 2 feet, to allow plenty of room for books and papers. The chair should be of such a height that your feet can be placed flat on the floor when your knees are at right angles. The seat height of men varies from 17–21 inches, and of women from 16–20 inches. Good office chairs are often adjustable over this range. The seat length from back to front is also important. Since the distance from the back of the buttocks to the back of the leg just below the knee varies from about 17–21 inches, a short seat will leave you with some of your thigh hanging uncomfortably over the edge of the seat, and a long seat will force you to sit away from the backrest or leave your legs dangling in the air.

The relation of chair height to height of the desk-top is also important. As you sit upright in the chair and let your arm hang vertically by your side the top of the desk should be about level with your elbow joint. You probably have to take your study furniture as you find it, but it may be possible to raise a desk that is too low by tacking wooden battens on the bottom of it, or counteracting a chair which is too high by using a footrest.

The advice about sitting tensed and upright does not, of course, mean that there is anything very wrong about reading a book in an easy chair. But where you have writing to do, or a difficult task to perform, you will do it better and more quickly at a desk than slumped in an easy chair or lying on a bed.

Noise and Work

Anyone who has had to do much intellectual work must at times have been distracted or even maddened by noise. With the evergrowing use of the internal combustion engine, noise is on the increase: bulldozers, aircraft and motor scooters sometimes seem to be sent to plague those who need quiet for study.

Yet the industrial psychologists tell us that noise has little effect on performance. Distracting noises at first reduce performance, but the worker can adjust to the noise fairly easily and return to his previous level of work. This is only true, however, of industrial work, and takes no account of the cost to the individual of maintaining concentration against a background of noise. Loud, discontinuous noises are the worst. Luckily we do become habituated to the lower levels of noise, and are able to shut them out from consciousness.

A distinction has to be made between "meaningless" noise and more meaningful sounds such as music or conversation. Meaningful sounds, although of less intensity, can obviously be much more distracting than sheer noise.

Noise, especially man-made noise, is a problem because little control over it is possible, short of wearing earplugs. Much depends on your attitude to the source of noise. I work a few hundred yards from a drop-forge which is seldom silent, and whose loud discontinuous clanging appalls most visitors. But it is possible to get used to it, and even to regard it with affection, by regarding it as a symbol of industry and national prosperity. The noises made by neighbors tend to be more upsetting, because they often seem to arise from lack of consideration and ignorance on the part of the neighbors.

In bad cases you may be able to insulate yourself from distracting noise by closing the windows and generating some sounds yourself, in order to mask the unwelcome noises from outside. A phonograph, for example, enables you to play music which you think is pleasant at intensities great enough to mask unwanted noises.

On the question of "music while you work" nothing very definite can be said. Experimental studies tend to show that the effects of music depend on attitudes to the music. Music can either increase or decrease performance, depending on whether you believe it to be an aid or a hindrance to your work. In industry its effect is greatest on boring and repetitive work. Since study is not usually either boring or repetitive it is unlikely to be assisted by music. In fact it is obvious that difficult mental work is best performed under quiet conditions.

Summary

You should pay careful attention to those aspects of the

physical environment that you can control. Artificial lighting should be of adequate intensity, well-distributed, and free from glare. Some form of indirect lighting is best.

When studying you should avoid stale and stuffy atmospheres. Good room ventilation is desirable. Many forms of room heating result in close conditions and lead to sleepiness.

You should work in a regular place, with books and materials at hand. But if you find it hard to settle to solitary work, working in libraries may be more effective.

Reasonably quiet conditions are desirable. But it is possible to adjust to the more moderate levels of noise. Much depends on the kind of noise and on your attitude to it.

For further reading:

Ryan, T. A., *Work and Effort*, Ronald Press, New York, 1947.

CHAPTER THIRTEEN

HEALTH AND STUDY

Hard students are commonly troubled with gouts, catarrhs, rheums, cachexia, bradypepsia, bad eyes, stones and colic, oppilations, vertigo, winds, consumptions, and all such diseases as come by overmuch sitting.

BURTON

WE can smile at Burton's catalogue of all the ailments which afflict "hard students", but he was undoubtedly correct in thinking that those who live a sedentary life of oversedulous study, and neglect bodily exercise, are likely to suffer from these multiple ailments, with the accompanying melancholy and discontent.

Without good health life is hardly worth living, and certainly no one can study effectively over a long period who is fatigued, sluggish, anemic or suffering from a succession of minor ailments. The need for mental health also (by which is meant freedom from worry and anxiety, a sense of self-worth, the ability to meet problems sensibly and rationally, the capacity for friendship and for enjoying life) demands that you should pay attention to your habits of exercise, sleep, diet, and to the physical environment in which you live, in so far as you can control it.

Youth, of course, is a healthy age, and young people with strong constitutions can tolerate all kinds of physical neglect without much immediate ill effect. Lack of exercise, in the view of some medical officers, is the most common fault; it has been estimated that about 40 per cent of men students and about 70 per cent of women students fail to take enough exercise.

Consider the physical environment of our industrial cities —the dirt, the smoke pall, the lack of fresh air and sunlight, the general lack of playgrounds and open spaces, and the ubiquitous bus and car, which relieve us of the necessity of walking. The sedentary life which civilization provides is clearly not ideal for physical health.

Body and mind are closely interrelated—more closely than is generally realized. Thinking, for example, is accompanied by slight muscular contractions. Work output is increased when the muscles are tensed—observe the bodily tension of someone who is working hard and concentrating. Emotions involve bodily changes, physical illnesses can result from anxiety, and organic disease causes psychological problems. Drugs cause simultaneous bodily and mental changes. The brain itself, the seat of consciousness, is entirely dependent on its blood supply. It is well supplied with blood vessels, a fine network of blood vessels actually encircling individual brain cells. The blood flow through the brain is faster than through most parts of the body, and the oxygen which the blood supplies is consumed in large quantities when the brain is active. If a part of the brain is temporarily deprived of blood, the brain cells are fatally injured in a few minutes. These facts should convince you that your powers of thought are likely to suffer when you are not in good bodily health, and they underline the need for oxygenation of the blood.

The effect of bodily condition on performance was well illustrated in an experiment by Mackworth at Cambridge. The number of mistakes made by two operators in receiving Morse messages was recorded when they were healthy and when they had head colds. In the healthy state they made very few mistakes. When they had colds their errors increased in consecutive messages until, by the ninth message received, one made over 100 mistakes and the other over 300.

Students' Ailments

The more frequent ailments from which students suffer are given in the table, which may be taken as fairly typical:

Dental decay	60–70 per cent
Frequent colds and respiratory infections, chronic nasal obstruction	20–30 ,, ,,
Minor accidents	15–20 ,, ,,
Skin troubles	14–16 ,, ,,
Digestive troubles	10–12 ,, ,,
Examination anxiety	5–10 ,, ,,
Uncorrected visual defects	5–10 ,, ,,

Some of these ailments may be unavoidable, others can be avoided, while most will yield to medical and dental treatment. A thorough medical examination is desirable before entering on a course of study, and indeed most universities and colleges now provide this service.

You yourself can practice a little preventive medicine. Dental decay will yield to regular dental treatment, a sensible diet, the toothbrush and the apple after meals. Colds can be avoided by keeping away from stuffy and overcrowded rooms, and by attending to focuses of infection in the nose and throat. Skin troubles may yield to diet, cleanliness and freedom from worry and anxiety. Digestive troubles can often be avoided by attention to diet and exercise. Examination anxiety does not usually trouble those who work regularly and are in good physical health.

The Need for Exercise

As has been said, some authorities think that 40 per cent of men and 70 per cent of women students fail to take sufficient exercise. It is of course difficult to define "sufficient exercise", and some individuals do need more or less exercise than others. There are in fact contrasting views about the value of exercise, and you should try and clarify your own ideas on this subject.

Is exercise good or can it be harmful? Some people, particularly those who are in poor physical condition after years of an inactive urban life, are afraid of the effects of exercise and wish to avoid unnecessary strain and effort. They think that exercise will only increase bodily wear and tear, and tell apocryphal stories of hale and hearty old men whose only exercise consists in helping to carry the coffins of their more energetic friends.

At the other extreme are those who think that natural selection, over thousands of years, has fitted the human body for strenuous activity in agriculture, hunting and war; and that those who live inactive sedentary lives in modern cities accumulate body-fat, lose muscular tone, and often worry excessively. In other words, muscles will atrophy unless they are used, and general bodily decay will be the result of inactivity and lack of exercise. There is, in fact, some medical evidence which suggests that those in sedentary occupations are less healthy than those in more active work. English bus conductors on double-decker buses are less likely to get coronary heart disease than the drivers. Walking postmen get less severe heart disease than postal office workers. Abnormalities of the heart in general are less common among active than among sedentary workers.

So, on purely physical grounds, there is very little doubt that some form of exercise, adapted to the needs of the individual, is beneficial. The real argument for exercise, however, is not that terrible things will happen to you if you don't take it, but that it is enjoyable for its own sake, and the best antidote for brooding and worrying. Jane Austen's heroines used to take a walk "in order to recover their spirits". Walking out of doors supplies novel stimuli for you to perceive and react to, starts new trains of thought, and the muscular activity itself can often lift one's mood. In many games you are forced to attend and react to a quick succession of stimuli, so that you are quite unable to think of anything but the immediate present, thus relieving you of any current worries or obsessions.

Exercise does not have to be in the form of strenuous competitive games and sports. Not everyone has an aptitude for athletics, and some probably avoid team games because they have never been good at them, or, because they learned to dislike them at school. The range of sports and active recreations is wide, however, including such relatively mild activities as walking, swimming, tennis, badminton, golf, dancing, skating, etc., so that everyone should be able to find some form of exercise, suited to his tastes and interests, which will take him away from his studies, and preferably into the open air, for at least one or two half days each week. At the University of Birmingham, England, all first-year students are required to take part in some form of organized physical activity each week. A wide choice of activities is offered, and most students, whatever their initial reactions to the scheme, enjoy themselves and learn new physical skills.

A habit of regular exercise is also desirable because, in the long run, the inactive tend to become overweight. This is, perhaps, a greater consideration in middle age than in youth. It seems that since the human body is adapted for activity, the sedentary almost inevitably eat more than they require. The mechanisms which regulate the intake of food allow an intake sufficient for a good deal of activity. Hence you must choose between activity, obesity, or, if you are determined enough to restrict your diet, feelings of semi-starvation.

It is common opinion, however, that it is not easy to lose weight by taking exercise. The energy value of food is measured in terms of calories. (A calorie is the amount of heat required to raise the temperature of a kilogram of water one degree centigrade.) The number of calories a person requires each day depends on his size and body weight, and on the amount of muscular work which he performs. A moderately active man weighing about 150 lb. probably needs about 2,500–3,000 calories daily. The caloric equivalent of 1 lb. of fats is about 36 hours' walking or about 10 hours' playing football. This makes it seem difficult to lose weight through exercise: you must walk for 36 hours in order to lose 1 lb. of body fat. Yet it is perfectly easy to walk for 36 hours in a month, which is still equivalent to a pound of body fat or to 12 lb. of body fat in the course of a year.

The following table will give you some idea of the energy cost of various forms of exercise in calories per hour.

	Calories per hour		Calories per hour
Walking 3 m.p.h.	250	Football	500
Running	800 or more	Rowing (at racing	
Cycling	700	speed)	1,000
Horse riding at		Swimming	500 or more
the trot	500	Squash	600
Dancing	300	Climbing	800
Golf	300	Wrestling	1,000
Tennis	400		

The daily food requirement for a person who is moderately active is 2,500–3,000 calories, but athletes may require up to twice these amounts. Roughly, 100 calories can be derived from ½ oz. butter, ¾ oz. chocolate, 1 oz. sugar or cheese, from 1½ oz. bread or 4 oz. of boiled potatoes. So you will have to walk for rather more than an hour to burn up the calories contained in 2 oz. of chocolate or 3 thick slices of bread. Nevertheless, regular exercise over a period is still a very effective way of avoiding obesity.

As a final argument, surveys show that on the average, those who are physically fit do better at their studies than those who are not: there is a correlation between physical fitness and academic marks. These results are perhaps what you would expect. Mental and physical fitness go together. Physical fitness is aided by appropriate exercise. Therefore, in the long run it will pay you to take exercise, not only for its own sake, but because it will help you indirectly in your studies.

Sleep

Eight hours of sleep each night are required by the average person. There is certainly a range of individual differences, but the vast majority take between six and nine hours' sleep. Presumably these figures refer to the hours when you are actually asleep and not to the hours when you are in bed. You probably have a fair idea from personal experience of how much sleep you need if you are to be at your best on the following day. Some are inclined to boast of how little sleep they need, and to point to the example of famous men, such as Napoleon or Edison, who apparently needed only a few hours' sleep each night. Scientific evidence, however, suggests that eminent men tend to sleep rather longer than others. Judging by the number of students who find it hard to get to early morning classes on time, there are many who either go to bed late or else spend more than eight hours in bed. Many individuals in fact work best on nine hours' sleep. Certainly there is no truth in the idea that only the first few hours of sleep are beneficial, and that the rest is wasted. At the same time most people do feel sluggish and lazy after oversleeping. Most feel at their best after a night's sleep which is no longer and no shorter than usual.

Sleep enables the body to eliminate the toxic products which have accumulated during the day, to repair damage to the tissues, and to store up energy. In sleep there is a decrease in the heart rate, a fall in blood pressure, and a change in the rhythm of the brain waves. The whole body is relaxed and rested in preparation for the next day's activity. This is perhaps not obvious to those who wake in the mornings feeling tired and out of sorts, and it is a fact that peak efficiency is not reached for some hours after rising. Consider, however, the effects of going without sleep. Animals kept without sleep for long periods will die, and prolonged loss of sleep is part of the technique of brainwashing.

Vigilance is not entirely lost in sleep. We are awakened by

unusual sounds. An elephant asleep will not wake when it is trodden on by another elephant, but will become alerted at the faintest unusual sound.

Rather surprisingly, experiments on students kept awake for up to 100 hours show that little decrement in performance results on either mental or physical tests. Much more effort than usual has to be expended, however, in order to maintain performance. The students became irritable, found difficulty in reading and writing, did not remember recent happenings, and suffered from headaches and dizziness. They were unable to maintain their alertness in tasks calling for continuous performance. Any kind of learning became very difficult. Smaller and lighter individuals generally suffered less than the stronger and more athletic.

Thus, although the effects of insomnia can be overcome in the short term by increased effort, in the long run efficiency is bound to suffer. In spite of the experimental evidence reported above, most people do feel fatigued after missing their normal sleep. This may be partly the result of suggestion, but it is also possible that, if more delicate measurements of the real cost of work to the individual were available, quite a small sleep loss could be shown to be detrimental to performance.

It is therefore important to establish regular habits of sleep and relaxation. Sleep is largely a matter of habit and physiological rhythm. Undressing, getting into bed, turning off the light, together with the freedom from noise and other distractions, constitute the conditioned stimuli for sleep. Their regular sequence is usually sufficient to ensure sleep when you are normally tired at the end of the day.

Yet there are times when it is difficult to get to sleep. The most common causes are unusual worry or excitement; unwise indulgence in food, coffee or tobacco; indigestion; lack of exercise; being too hot or too cold; and attempting to wrangle with intellectual problems too near to bedtime. It is usually wise to avoid intense mental activity immediately before going to bed—otherwise confused dreams and restlessness may result. It is best to relax, and talk or read some light work. Reading in bed often induces sleep, since it is fatiguing and produces eyestrain.

Deep, unbroken sleep is more wholesome and refreshing than light and fitful sleeping. Is there anything that can be done to improve the quality of sleep? The type of bed, whether hard or soft, probably has little to do with the type of sleep. The ideal bed is probably that which allows movement during sleep. The average sleeper changes his posture every eleven minutes. Men are more mobile than women (as many aggrieved wives are aware). It seems that no one position or posture will give maximum rest to all parts of the body. Hence movement is necessary to relieve the tensions and cramps which arise in any particular posture. As many as fifty changes of posture are made in the course of a normal night's sleep, in order to relax each part of the body in turn. It is said that you can sleep just as soundly on boards or on the ground as on an inner spring mattress—provided that you are used to doing so. Sleeping on boards, however, tends to make certain postures extremely uncomfortable, so there is something to be said for having a bed soft enough to allow you to turn all round during sleep without discomfort.

Diet

Healthy people do not worry very much about what they eat. But there are many otherwise quite sensible persons who have aversions to such valuable foods as milk, fish, tomatoes, etc., and a fair number of faddists who live on very restricted diets. Most of us are probably rather too rigid and conservative in our choice of foods: definite preferences for certain classes of food seem to be established in childhood, so that we habitually, and sometimes unwisely, consume certain foods, and neglect others.

Food provides energy for work and for the vital functions of the body. It helps to make good bodily wear and tear, and it supplies "fuel" for the maintenance of body heat. Few people in the West today go short of calories, but the calories may be derived from an excessive intake of sugar and processed cereals, so that other important dietary elements are lacking. The staple diet of paupers has always been white bread, sugar and potatoes, which supply the calories, but not the proteins, minerals and vitamins essential for health. In order to preserve health, a diet must contain proteins, fats, carbohydrates, minerals, vitamins and water, in proper proportions.

The elements most likely to be deficient are calcium and vitamins A and C, and further, in diets containing a great deal of sugar and processed cereals, protein, iron and vitamin B_1. Lack of energy and vitality are thought to result from mild vitamin deficiencies. The following table indicates which food substances are good sources (although not of course the only sources) of the important vitamins and minerals:

Minerals and Vitamins	Good Sources	Deficiency Symptoms
A Important in growth Stored in body	Fish liver (cod liver oil) Some yellow and green vegetables (e.g. carrots, water cress) Ox and sheep liver Butter	Eye discomfort Poor night vision Poor hearing Dryness of skin Frequent colds
B₁ (aneurin)	Yeast Cereal germs Liver Egg yolk	Loss of appetite Lack of energy Constipation
B₂ (riboflavin)	Yeast Liver Milk and cheese Eggs Fish roe	Rough skin Cracking of skin at corners of mouth
Nicotinic acid (Niacin) Antipellagra	Liver Yeast Meat Wholewheat flour	Dermatitis Mental depression
C (ascorbic acid) Anti-scurvy Destroyed by cooking and drying Not stored in body	Rose hips Black currants Strawberries Citrus fruits Green vegetables especially the cabbage family (not lettuce) Tomatoes	Boils Failure of wounds to heal Fatigue, anemia

Minerals and Vitamins	Good Sources	Deficiency Symptoms
D Stored in body	Sunshine Fish liver oils Herring Mackerel Sardines Eggs	Rickets Poor calcification of bones Dental decay

Minerals	Good Sources	Deficiency Symptoms
Calcium Important for bone development	Sardines Cheese, cream Egg yolk Celery, beans Almonds Dried figs Water cress	Bad teeth Nose bleeding
Phosphorus Essential in all body chemistry	Cheese Sardines Eggs Fish Oatmeal Beans	Poor appetite Loss of weight
Iron Essential for formation of hemoglobin in red blood corpuscles	Heart, liver Eggs Oatmeal Black currants Dried fruits Cocoa and chocolate	Anemia Low vitality
Iodine Essential for thyroid functions	Fish Broccoli Iodized salt	Low metabolism Susceptibility to infection

It is difficult to assess the exact amounts of vitamins and minerals required, and you must not jump to the conclusion that the deficiency symptoms listed fit your own particular case. The effects of vitamins depend on other components in the diet, and on their inter-relationship. For instance Vitamin D can be antagonized by an unsatisfactory calcium-phosphorus intake. An excess of carbohydrate in the diet necessitates an increase in the intake of Vitamin B_1. The vitamin B units are closely interrelated in their action.

If you pass your eye quickly down the table of vitamins and minerals you will see that certain foodstuffs appear several times in the table, and are therefore particularly valuable. Some of these are eggs, liver, raw green vegetables, tomatoes, milk, cheese, fish and wholewheat bread.

Since the most likely deficiencies are of Vitamins A and C and calcium, and possibly Vitamin B_1 and iron, you should ensure that you get enough of the foodstuffs mentioned as good sources of these elements, particularly in the late winter. In winter, the vitamin content of foods declines. Early potatoes may have 8 mg. of vitamin C per oz., old stored potatoes only 1 mg. per oz. Summer milk may have 800 international units of vitamin A per pint, winter milk less than half that amount. Many students have to eat at large cafeterias and canteens in which food may be kept on hot plates for some hours. This has the effect of destroying what little vitamin C may be left over from the cooking.

Because of the difficulties of getting enough vitamin C in the winter diet at a reasonable cost, it may be worth supplementing your diet with synthetic vitamins. This is best done, however, by taking a complete supplement, consisting of all the important vitamins and minerals listed above, not by taking tablets of the one element you think is missing from your diet. Complete supplements are readily available commercially. Probably quite small doses are effective—much smaller than the makers usually recommend.

There is no evidence that increasing either vitamins B or C in the diet beyond normal levels improves either the work performance or the resistance to fatigue of young healthy adults. But vitamin supplements apparently help to cut down minor ailments. In a study on a group of aircraft workers in California in the last world war, an experimental group was given a vitamin supplement five days a week for a year. A control group was given 'placebo' pills, and a third group no treatment at all. The vitamin group proved to be superior to the other two groups in working efficiency over the year.

Remember, however, that vitamin supplements are only supplements, and in no sense substitutes for fresh fruit and vegetables, milk, cheese, eggs, liver, fish and other protective foods.

A good diet will include daily:

1. Tomatoes, oranges, raw cabbage or salad—one or more servings.
2. Other vegetables or fruits—one or more servings.
3. Meat or fish—one or more servings.
4. Eggs—one a day.
5. Cereals and bread—including some wholewheat bread.
6. Butter or vitamin-enriched margarine.
7. Cheese—one serving.
8. Milk—at least 1 pint.
9. Water, or beverages containing water—2½–3 pints.

The best way of ensuring that your diet contains all the necessary vitamins is to eat a good variety of foods. Make sure that you spend adequate amounts on:

Vegetables and fruit.
Milk and cheese.
Meat, fish and eggs.

I shall summarize this discussion by listing those foods that I think sedentary workers should eat more of, and those that they should eat less of. In the main they should eat less starchy food, and more fruit, vegetables and proteins. Athletes, and those doing heavy muscular work, on the other hand, need to consume large amounts of carbohydrate to supply fuel for their muscles.

Foods that sedentary workers should eat more of:	*Food that sedentary workers should eat less of:*
Raw shredded cabbage and grated carrots	Sugar
Water cress	Cakes, biscuits and pastries and other sugary confectionery
Tomatoes	
Oranges and other fresh fruit	Candies
Ox and sheep liver	Processed meats and pies

Foods that sedentary workers should eat more of:	Foods that sedentary workers should eat less of:
Eggs	Made up and rehashed meat dishes
Cheese and dairy products	Sausages
Fresh herrings, sardines, cod's roe	Packeted breakfast cereals
Oatmeal	Canned foods
Yeast extracts	Beer
Nuts and dried fruits	

Finally, a word about how you take your meals. Bacon said: "To be free-minded and cheerfully disposed at hours of meat . . . is one of the best precepts of long lasting." Avoid hurry and anxiety at mealtimes—they interfere with digestion. This may sound like a counsel of perfection if you are sometimes forced to take a hasty snack, or to join a long line for meals, but the ideal is to be able to sit relaxed, among friends with whom you feel at ease.

Alcohol

Alcohol depresses all psychological functions and reduces general efficiency. In spite of the overwhelming scientific evidence for this statement, many people nevertheless regard alcohol as a stimulant. Many habitual drinkers declare that a few drinks excite rather than fatigue them, and increase their efficiency rather than depress it. How is this conflict between popular belief and scientific evidence to be explained? The answer seems to be that even quite small doses of alcohol have a depressant effect on the central nervous system as a whole, including the brain. An important function of the highest centers of the brain is to inhibit the expression of emotion and impulse, and to supply intellectual control and self-criticism. One of the first and most obvious effects of alcohol is to destroy this intellectual control: after a few drinks there is often a sense of well-being, feelings of comradeship towards fellow drinkers, an increase in self-confidence and loss of timidity. Tongues begin to wag, there is much boasting and loud talk, pet hatreds and prejudices are freely expressed, and after more drinks, many are prone to sentimental weepings, outbursts of anger and uninhibited sexual behavior, as the primary emotions are freed from their normal cerebral control.

So, although alcohol sometimes appears to the drinker to be a stimulant because of the loss of self-criticism, its actual effect is to depress most bodily and mental functions. Its immediate effects on the person will vary with body-weight, the state of the stomach, the concentration of the alcohol and the rate at which it is ingested. Habitual drinkers build up a tolerance for alcohol, so that they are not as much affected by small amounts of alcohol as those who seldom drink. Degree of intoxication nevertheless largely depends on the amount of alcohol in the blood. The usual course of intoxication may be presented facetiously thus:

Alcohol in Blood:

0.05% or 0.10% less	0.18%	0.22%	0.32%	0.4%	0.5%
Dry and decent.	Delighted and devilish.	Delinquent and disgusting.	Dizzy and delirious.	Dazed and dejected.	Dead drunk.	Dead.

It hardly needs to be said that alcohol, even in small amounts, is likely to interfere with study. In one experiment weak beer (2.75 per cent of alcohol) was drunk on certain days, and beer from which the alcohol had been removed on other days. Tests were made of physical functions before and after drinking, and also of speed of adding and speed of learning. All the psychological tests showed some decrement in performance after drinking alcohol.

The graph on the facing page shows a typical result: speed of adding was much reduced after a few weak beers in the lunch break.

On the physical side, alcohol sends up the pulse rate. The heart rate increases, not because of any stimulating effect, but because alcohol, like nicotine, interferes with the operation of the vagus nerve, which normally slows down the heart rate. Alcohol also produces an illusory sensation of warmth. This is because alcohol causes a relaxation of the walls of the blood vessels, allowing easy circulation of the blood in the skin areas. Heat is thus radiated freely from the body, and the actual body temperature therefore drops.

In view of these facts, you may wonder why most human societies use alcohol on social occasions, festivals, birthdays, weddings and funerals. The reason is that alcohol promotes what the sociologists call "informal social integration", i.e. feelings of unity, friendship and solidarity with one's fellows.

Moreover, a drinking "culture" arises, in learned institutions as elsewhere, with definite rituals for preparing drinks, imbibing them, drinking songs, drinking contests, together with their associated stories and legends. Men students, in particular, may find that drinking on special occasions is a common way of cementing friendships, and sometimes a kind of protest and escape from the hardships of student life.

Studies show that about 80 per cent of men and 60 per cent of women students drink, but that only 20 per cent of men

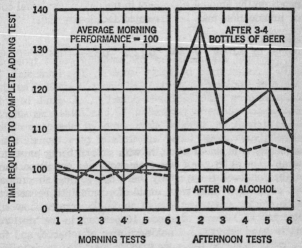

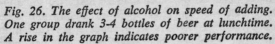

Fig. 26. The effect of alcohol on speed of adding. One group drank 3-4 bottles of beer at lunchtime. A rise in the graph indicates poorer performance.

and 10 per cent of women drink more frequently than once a week. For a normal well-balanced person there is obviously very little harm in taking a few drinks on a Saturday night. For unstable personalities, on the other hand, alcohol provides such a ready means of escape from personal difficulties and limitations that they may be unable to be moderate in their use of alcohol.

In summary, to drink even small quantities of alcohol is ill-advised on those days on which you mean to do hard intellectual work. The more difficult and the more "creative" the task, the worse will be the effect of alcohol. The great German physiologist, Helmholtz, thought that even tiny amounts of alcohol ruined his intellectual creativity. Those people who claim that alcohol helps them to work have built up a tolerance for it by daily drinking. So unless you wish to build up a tolerance by regular indulgence, it is clearly much better not to drink on working days. At the convivial party or special occasion, each individual probably has to learn from unpleasant experience sensible limits which he should not exceed. At all events it is stupid to drink so much that hangovers, illness and unfitness for work follow the next day.

Tobacco

The principal arguments against smoking result from the health risks incurred by heavy smokers. The immediate influence of smoking on working efficiency is small. The classic research on this subject was done by C. L. Hull. In order to avoid the effects of suggestion, he blindfolded his subjects and gave them, on "tobacco" days, a pipe of tobacco to smoke, and on "tobaccoless days" an artificial pipe though which warm moist air was sucked, tobacco smoke being present in the air. The subjects of the experiment did not suspect that on the tobaccoless days they were not getting an ordinary pipe of tobacco: they were unable to distinguish between tobacco smoke and warm moist air. Hull's results show that there was an increase of almost 10 per cent in the heart rate and in hand tremor on smoking a pipe of tobacco, and that this effect persisted for more than an hour. On some tests of working efficiency, such as speed of adding and speed of learning, habitual smokers were about 5 per cent more efficient after smoking, but those who did not normally smoke were about 3 per cent less efficient after smoking. On most of the functions tested, however, the differences were unreliable and inconsistent, showing that smoking has a negligible effect on work.

The nicotine in tobacco is a poison and makes a very effective insecticide. Both cigarettes and intravenous injections of nicotine have the same effects: an increase in heart rate, in blood pressure and in basal metabolism. Many people put on weight when they give up smoking, partly because their metabolism is slightly reduced, and partly because they eat more.

On the positive side smoking is supposed to allay anxiety

and provide relief from tension. It encourages sociability and provides the idle with an occupation.

As a group, nonsmokers are better students than smokers. This difference in performance, however, probably has nothing to do with smoking as such. Smokers tended to be more sociable than nonsmokers, and therefore to be rather more likely to neglect their work than nonsmokers.

The now notorious association of heavy smoking not only with lung cancer, but also with bronchitis and coronary heart disease, suggests that it is advisable not to exceed ten cigarettes a day, to use filters and not to smoke cigarettes down to the last inch; and better still not to smoke at all. The death rate from lung cancer in the U.S.A. is estimated at 127 per 100,000 per year from cigarette smokers, 39 per 100,000 for pipe smokers and 13 per 100,000 for nonsmokers. These facts have suggested to many men that a pipe is safer than cigarettes.

Caffeine

The stimulant drug, caffeine, is contained in some form in tea, coffee and cocoa. A large cup of tea or coffee contains about 2½ grains of caffeine. In small and moderate doses (1–4 grains) caffeine improves most mental performances. In larger doses it may have a depressant effect, and, in doses of 6 grains or more it interferes with sleep. It does not increase ability, but makes the person more awake, less fatigued and quicker to react.

Tea and coffee are drunk by almost everyone, and if they have any harmful or toxic effects on the system, these are not obvious. These beverages are, however, habit-forming: many individuals are difficult to live with until they have had their morning cup, and to be deprived of the habitual eleven o'clock tea or coffee causes psychological unrest. William Cobbett used to inveigh against the injurious effects of "tea, coffee and other slop-kettle". In small doses, however, caffeine does not seem to produce any harmful effects in the body, other than causing a great increase in tremor and a loss of muscular steadiness, while it does make for heightened efficiency, the stimulating effect occurring after about 2 hours and lasting until the following day.

Tea and coffee, then, are fairly harmless stimulants. Some students take tablets of caffeine citrate in order to stay awake late and work for examinations. This practice is not to be recommended, since large doses interfere with sleep and relaxation.

The drug benzedrine sulphate has an even more marked effect in relieving symptoms of fatigue, and unlike caffeine, it increases muscular steadiness. It has been successfully used to combat fatigue in military operations, and is sometimes given clandestinely to race horses. It can only be obtained on medical prescription, however, and this is wise since in the long run the loss of sleep resulting from taking the drug would lower performance.

Summary

Body and mind are closely related, and mental efficiency is affected by the state of the body.

Many students fail to take sufficient exercise. Evidence is quoted that the physically active enjoy better health than the sedentary, and that students who are in good health do better than those in poor health.

Although loss of sleep may have little effect on work in the short term, it is important to establish sound habits of sleep and relaxation.

Diets may be deficient in important vitamins and minerals, especially in winter. You should make sure that your diet contains adequate amounts of fresh fruit and vegetables, milk, cheese, eggs, liver, fish and other protective foods.

Alcohol depresses all psychological functions and should be avoided on working days.

Tobacco has little effect on working efficiency, but heavy smoking is associated with lung cancer, bronchitis and heart disease.

The caffeine contained in tea and coffee, although habit forming, is a harmless stimulant.

For further reading:

Johnson, W. R. (Ed.), *Science and Medicine of Exercise and Sports*, Harper, New York, 1960.

Cruickshank, E. H. W., *Food and Nutrition*, E. & S. Livingstone, Edinburgh, 1951.

CHAPTER FOURTEEN

MENTAL HEALTH

It is too frequently the pride of students to despise those amusements and recreations which give to the rest of mankind strength of limbs and cheerfulness of heart.

JOHNSON

JUST as you can improve your physical health by attention to diet, exercise and sleep, so you can improve your mental health by intelligent self-direction. But the most effective self-direction is of an indirect sort, and usually means building up friendships and activities, not ruminating about the self. Lengthy self-analysis, excessive self-consciousness and overconcern with one's own difficulties are morbid activities, and seldom lead to any personal improvement. The common advice to "leave your mind alone", is good advice in the sense that a day's outdoor exercise with friends is usually a much better remedy against conflict and anxiety than a period of solitary brooding.

At the same time all resourceful people think about their experiences, and try and learn from them. Although your personality is determined by the past—by the complicated interplay of heredity and social training—you are still free to choose between courses of action. Although no one can, in a short space of time, bring about radical changes in his behavior or overcome personal limitations—indeed psychologists work on the assumption that behavior is determined by past experience—you can at least learn not to repeat past mistakes. The intelligent person learns to look at the alternatives before him, to consider their probable consequences, and to choose those courses of action which are likely to lead to desirable results.

This final chapter will deal with the achievement motive, with social participation, with reactions to thwarting, and

with sex. On few of these matters can any definite advice be
given, but I hope that the account given here may give you
occasional fresh insights into your behavior.

The Achievement Motive

Societies like ours, in which careers are supposed to be open
to talent, encourage competitive striving for success. When
social position and advancement depend on effort, parents
begin very early to put pressure on their children to work
hard at school. Striving for success begins in school, and
later, in a whole range of white-collar occupations success
depends on passing a series of competitive examinations, and
on being promoted from one salary level to the next.

For success in most branches of study you must have definite vocational aims and high personal ambition. In one research study the following questionnaire items were found
to distinguish between over-achievers (in relation to intelligence) and under-achievers:

(1) Planning only makes a person unhappy since your plans
    hardly ever work out anyhow. (Over-achievers disagree;
    under-achievers agree.)
(2) When a man is born, the success he's going to have is al-
    ready in the cards, so he might as well accept it and not
    fight against it. (Over-achievers disagree; under-achievers
    agree.)
(3) The best kind of job to have is one where you are part of
    an organization all working together even if you don't
    get individual credit. (Over-achievers disagree; under-
    achievers agree.)
(4) When the time comes for a boy to take a job, he should
    stay near his parents, even if it means giving up a good
    job opportunity. (Over-achievers disagree; under-achiev-
    ers agree.)
(5) It's silly for a teenager to put money into a car when the
    money could be used to get started in business or for an
    education. (Over-achievers agree; under-achievers dis-
    agree.)
(6) Nowadays, with world conditions what they are, the wise
    person lives for today and lets tomorrow take care of it-
    self. (Over-achievers disagree; under-achievers agree.)

You can see that the over-achievers believe in planning and

effort and working towards distant goals, that they are prepared to move away from home, and that they would prefer jobs in which individual merit is recognized. Planning, effort and working towards long-term goals have been recommended throughout this book. But you should remember also that an excessively high level of motivation can interfere with intellectual performance. Moreover, success may be attained at too great a cost if the person turns into an anxious "striver" in the process. A life of grim and exhausting work may lead to public success but to personal failure. It is only too obvious that many of those who attain high office have reached their place after labors which have left them no time to develop much social or practical intelligence. Worse still, overconcern with reputation and success blights all relationships with others, since others are seen as rivals, or are merely manipulated or exploited for personal ends.

The egocentric person, without ordinary human sympathy, is, in Bacon's words, "a busy mischievous, wretched thing, no better than a kind of vermin". Unfortunately the hierarchical organization of industrial society tends to reward egocentric strivers after power, as witness the absurd pretensions and status-consciousness of many "organization men".

Social Participation

Both the very sociable and the very unsociable make poor students. On the one hand those who spend a great part of their time in convivial parties or in idle conversation fail to do enough work. On the other hand the social isolates who take no part in student activities often fail in their work because they lack the stimulus and help of friends. Some psychologists look upon extent of social participation as some index of a person's mental health. It certainly is some index of the person's energy and activity, since friendships are based on some kind of shared activity, in work, sports or recreation; and the more activities a person engages in, the more friendships he is likely to make. Since man is a social animal, he needs good social relations with others. But social needs are stronger in some than in others. Some people would sooner have solitude and contemplation than a noisy round of social life, and there is no evidence that such people need be "maladjusted". There is no virtue in spending a great deal of time in idle chatter and gossip.

The highest academic honors are sometimes won by those

who are rather unsociable, and more interested in books and ideas than in other people. There is indeed some evidence that the labors of an academic course are best tolerated by those who, on general psychological grounds, might be regarded as having mildly pathological characteristics, such as social withdrawal, and rigid control of emotion. This evidence, however, is merely an indictment of courses of study which encourage these pathological tendencies. Ordinary social competence, on general grounds, is just as important as academic success, and this social competence can only be achieved by adequate practice in many different social roles.

The spate of popular literature on how to win friends and influence people is avidly read by salesmen and others whose idea of friendship is to manipulate others for their own advantage. Its cardinal principle is that you should praise and flatter others and pretend an interest in their concerns so that they will like you. Such hypocritical praise and flattery is bound to be seen as false in the long term, yet this "sales" advice does contain an element of truth: friends are aware of each other's needs and purposes, and give each other mutual support. Friendships depend on shared interests and activities. No friendships last unless the friends work together or associate in their pleasures and recreations.

The factors which influence the formation of friendships are not well understood. Similarity of experience, taste and opinions are obviously important, but some friendships are complementary, as when a dominant person forms a friendship with a subservient person. Everyone feels attracted to some individuals more than others, and sometimes the basis of attraction seems to defy conscious analysis. Some are benevolently inclined to people in general; others tend to be hostile to others. Some form a few deep friendships, others a larger number of superficial relationships.

Difficulties in interpersonal relationships are usually the result of egocentricity—an overconcern with your own problems—and feelings of hostility toward others, many of which stem from dissatisfaction with the self. Excessive striving for power and status, as has been said above, makes genuine friendship difficult. Those in power and authority are usually esteemed rather than liked, at any rate by those in lesser positions.

Social competence comes easily to those who are healthy, intelligent, and sympathetic towards others. Such people do not regard others with suspicion or dislike. They respect confidences and avoid malicious gossip.

Reactions to Thwarting *

Reaction	This action is likely when—	This action is desirable when—	This action is undesirable when—
Repetitive response	Person expects response to succeed. Person cannot withdraw or reinterpret, or dislikes trying the more appropriate response.	Person reexamines situation before deciding to repeat.	Person is "forcing" without reexamination. Repetition is long continued.
Altered response	Person has little faith in his original response. Person has confidence in his ability to reinterpret and carry out a new action.	The new response is based on reinterpretation; the old response is given due consideration.	New response is chosen thoughtlessly.
Withdrawal	Person does not expect to succeed. Person finds trying unpleasant, or does not value the goal.	Person has little chance of succeeding. Goal is unimportant.	Person withdraws when reasonable effort will bring success.
Substitution	Substitute is available. Other conditions as in withdrawing	The new goal satisfies the same needs as the original goal. The new goal permits useful learning. Other conditions as in withdrawing.	Person fails to satisfy a basic need, so develops in unbalanced manner. Person must learn to cope with original situation. The substitute undertaking is unrealistic.

Reactions to Failure

From the earliest days of life everyone has to learn that needs cannot always be satisfied, and that desires are not always attained. When faced with failures and difficulties there are four courses of action open to you:

(1) You can repeat the same kind of behavior which has resulted in failure, in the hope that next time you will be successful.

* From L. J. Cronbach, *Educational Psychology*, 2nd Edn., Harcourt, Brace and World Inc., New York, 1963, p. 585.

(2) You can vary behavior, using a different method of attack on the obstacles before you.

(3) You can give up trying and take no further action.

(4) You can give up trying to reach your original goal, but work towards some other goal as a substitute or compensatory activity.

The traditional precept to "keep trying" does often ensure that difficulties and obstacles will be overcome. But it is not always the most intelligent response. It is usually better to analyze the reasons for failure, and to make a rational appraisal of the four possibilities of action. Each may be the most appropriate reaction, depending on the situation. The table on page 233 gives some indication of the circumstances in which the four kinds of reaction are desirable and undesirable.

Sex

The sexual drive in men is much higher than is necessary for procreation, and it reaches its peak in the adolescent years, well before marriage. Most young men therefore have the difficult problem of dealing with unresolved sexual tensions. The rates of sexual "outlet" of all kinds, including nocturnal emissions, were found by Kinsey, in his large-scale study of American men to be, for males under 30 years:

Frequency of outlet per week	Percentage
0 or less than 0.5	3.7
0.5 – 1.0	22.1
1.5 – 2.5	30.9
3.0 – 4.5	25.9
5.0 – 7.5	12.2
8.0 and more	5.2

The median frequency is about two outlets weekly, but there is a considerable range of individual differences.

In women the sexual drive is less strong, and the nature of "outlet" is less clear, but Kinsey states that only about one third of women come up to the male average before marriage.

The wide range of individual differences is the result of the interplay of many factors, among which can be distinguished:

(1) Physiological and hormonal factors.
(2) Habits and past experience of sexual activity.
(3) Social rules and restraints.
(4) External stimulation, including the availability of sexual partners.

The highest rates of activity will be found amongst those who are endowed with a high degree of sexual vigor, who have built up habits of indulgence, who are uninfluenced by social controls, and who have sexual partners readily available. Such are some of Kinsey's criminals and "underworld" men.

The lowest rates will be found amongst those who have weak sexual drives, who have never indulged in much sexual activity, whose moral and religious beliefs condemn it, and who live in an environment in which sexual partners are not available. Such might be celibate priests.

All human societies put some restraints on sexual activity, and these tend to be most severe in Protestant countries. All Western societies restrain sexual activity, not only to avoid unwanted pregnancies and the spread of disease, but also because promiscuity would undermine their forms of marriage and family life. For the individual, excessive sexual activity usually means the dissipation of energies which might be devoted to more useful purposes. The demands of work and study are met with less possibility of conflict by those who have rather a low level of sexual response—most courses of study imply a prolonged period of economic dependence, and the postponement of marriage.

An important question is whether the energy which might be given to sex can or should be channeled into other activities. It is a common idea that the highest achievements depend on suppressing direct sexual activity and directing energy to higher ends. But Freud himself thought that such "sublimation" was found in many people only in slight degree. Kinsey was frankly contemptuous of the idea of sublimation, and thought that, apart from those who were physically incapable or natively low in sex drive, there were simply no cases of sublimation in his studies. Similarly a study of forty healthy young unmarried men at Harvard University, whose character and achievements were of the highest order, showed that all habitually engaged in direct sexual activity of some kind. It would appear therefore, that few men are able to attain absolute continence, at least in our modern society, in which sex tends to be overvalued, commercially exploited, and regarded as a desirable activity in itself. This is not to say that the level of sexual activity cannot be lowered by directing interests elsewhere, by taking strenuous physical exercise, and by avoiding those situations which are likely to stimulate sexual activity.

The discussion of sex may seem to be too crudely biological to do justice to the romanticism which surrounds the relationship between the sexes, but does nevertheless present the crux of the matter: that men students in particular have to control their sexual drives, and since direct heterosexual gratification is seldom possible, to direct their interests to their work as far as possible, and to get by with such partial or substitute satisfactions as will be least damaging to their self-respect.

Summary

High achievement comes from strong ambitions. But the competitive struggle for success can lead to too high a level of motivation. Don't allow the success ideology to turn you into an anxious striver.

In some branches of study the most able students may be somewhat unsociable and withdrawn. But academic success should not be won at the price of ordinary social competence. Sources of difficulty in interpersonal relations are listed.

There are four general reactions to failure: repeated effort, a new kind of effort, withdrawal, and substitute activity. The kinds of situation are outlined in which each of these reactions may be appropriate.

Men students, in particular, tend to be faced with the problem of dealing with unresolved sexual tensions. These should not cause personal conflict if the individual realizes that his situation is common to most others in his age group.

For further reading:
Coleman, J. C., *Personality Dynamics and Effective Behavior*, Scott, Foresman and Co., Chicago, 1960.

Index